Virgil A. Walker

Why Many Evangelicals Are Not Protestant: The Creedless Drift

Written By Virgil A. Walker

Published by House Walker Publishing

Why Many Evangelicals are Not Protestant: The Creedless Drift

Published by House Walker Publishing

Copyright © 2025 Virgil A. Walker

All rights reserved. No part of this publication may be reproduced, distributed, or transmitted in any form or by any means, including photocopying, recording, or other electronic or mechanical methods, without the prior written permission of the author, except in the case of brief quotations embodied in critical reviews and certain other noncommercial uses permitted by copyright law.

Virgil A. Walker

Introduction 4

Chapter 1: The Reformation's Communal, Confessional Vision 11

Chapter 2: Early Radicals: Paulicians, Bogomils, and the Seeds of Dissent 24

Chapter 3: Theological Drift: From Sola Scriptura to Solo Spirituality 35

Chapter 4: Radical Fringes: Polygamy as a Symptom of Departure 51

Chapter 5: Cultural Conformity: Radicalism Masquerading as Relevance 59

Chapter 6: Can Evangelicalism Reclaim Historic Christianity? 68

Conclusion 77

Call to Action 85

About the Author 86

Glossary 87

Bibliography 94

Why Many Evangelicals are Not Protestant: The Creedless Drift

Introduction

Imagine Martin Luther stepping into a modern megachurch, stage lights flashing and worship music pulsing through the air. Would he see the fruit of his Reformation—a movement rooted in biblical authority, confessional rigor, and communal faith? Or would he encounter something unrecognizable, a spectacle more akin to the radical Anabaptist gatherings he denounced as chaotic? Picture Dietrich Bonhoeffer, who warned against "cheap grace," sitting through a sermon promising personal fulfillment over costly discipleship. Would he recognize the faith he defended—or a drift toward the individualistic tendencies of the Paulicians and Bogomils?

These questions drive this book. Modern evangelicalism, particularly in its Pentecostal and nondenominational expressions, has undergone a profound shift. What began as a Protestant movement grounded in the Reformation's principles—sola scriptura (Scripture alone), disciplined worship, and a covenantal community—has, in some quarters, become something the reformers would scarcely recognize. By "Protestant," I mean the historic denominations birthed or shaped by the Reformation: Lutheran, Presbyterian, Anglican, Reformed, Congregationalist, Methodist, and Baptist, though some

Virgil A. Walker

Baptist stances overlap with evangelical trends. In contrast, the nondenominational and Pentecostal strands of evangelicalism often elevate personal experience, cultural relevance, and individual autonomy above the historic markers of Christian faith: creeds, sacraments, and ecclesiastical accountability. I propose that this shift, in certain contexts, is not mere adaptation but a departure from Reformation Protestantism, echoing the individualism of radical dissenters like the Paulicians, Bogomils, and Anabaptists—movements the reformers viewed as schismatic.

Let me be clear: this book is not an attack on evangelicals. Evangelicals are individuals with their own individual beliefs, many whom I affirm as brothers and sisters in Christ. Many evangelicals, especially within confessional Protestant denominations, such as Reformed evangelicals and Anglican evangelicals for example, who faithfully uphold the gospel and Reformation ideals. My concern lies with specific trends—particularly in nondenominationalism and Pentecostalism—that risk undermining the unity Christ prayed for in John 17:20–23, when He asked that His followers "be one" as He and the Father are one. Nondenominationalism, with its rejection of denominational ties and historic confessions, often fosters a "just me and my Bible" mindset that I believe is unbiblical, as it sidesteps the communal accountability

Why Many Evangelicals are Not Protestant: The Creedless Drift

Christ's prayer envisions. Creeds and confessions, like the Nicene and Apostles' Creeds or the Augsburg and Westminster Confessions, are not mere human traditions but unifying bonds, enabling diverse denominations—Lutheran, Presbyterian, Baptist, and beyond—to confess one faith as different provinces in the Kingdom of God. These guardrails ensure we remain anchored to Scripture within the church's shared witness, despite our differences. Regardless of doctrinal differences amount us, I strive to be ecumenical with all my fellow brethren in Christ. But it is important to define what makes one a Christian and who are the pretenders.

This book is a call to reflection, not division. I invite evangelicals, particularly those in nondenominational and Pentecostal circles, to consider whether their practices align with the Reformation's communal vision or echo the radical autonomy of historical dissenters. By drawing parallels to groups like the Anabaptists, I am not labeling evangelicals as heretics but highlighting tendencies that concerned reformers like Luther, Calvin, and even more modern examples like Bonhoeffer. My aim is to spark dialogue about evangelicalism's trajectory and its fidelity to Protestant roots.

Defining the Terms

To grasp this transformation, we must clarify our terms. Historic Christianity, as it emerged over centuries, is defined by communal worship, sacramental theology, and adherence to ecumenical creeds like the Nicene and Apostles' Creeds. Reformation Protestantism, embodied in the seven denominations noted above, preserved this communal and confessional core while correcting Catholic abuses. Luther, Calvin, and their heirs emphasized sola scriptura but interpreted Scripture within the church's tradition and authority, producing confessions to guide the faithful. Theirs was a faith of structure, discipline, and community.

Modern evangelicalism, particularly in its nondenominational and Pentecostal forms, often departs from this vision. Personal conversion, emotional worship, and individual interpretation dominate, with creeds sidelined as relics and denominational ties viewed with skepticism. This turn toward individualism has historical parallels—ones that predate the Reformation and alarmed its leaders.

Echoes of Radical Dissent

Consider the Paulicians, a 7th-century sect in Armenia and Byzantium. They rejected the Byzantine church's hierarchy and sacraments, favoring a simplified, individualistic faith centered on Paul's epistles. The

Why Many Evangelicals are Not Protestant: The Creedless Drift

Bogomils, influenced by the Paulicians, embraced dualism, rejecting the material world—including church buildings and rituals—for a subjective spirituality. Fast forward to the Reformation: the Anabaptists, admired today for their believer's baptism, were seen by Luther and Calvin as dangerous radicals. Luther's *Against the Heavenly Prophets* (1525) and Calvin's *Treatise Against the Anabaptists* (1544) condemned their rejection of church authority and subjective scriptural interpretations as schismatic. These groups, though varied, shared a disdain for institutional constraints, prioritizing personal or communal autonomy—a pattern that resurfaces in modern evangelicalism.

Pentecostalism's focus on personal spiritual gifts, like speaking in tongues, and nondenominationalism's creedless, market-driven worship mirror these radical tendencies. This isn't to label all evangelicals as heretics—far from it. But their practices and priorities have shifted so far from Reformation Protestantism that they align more with the Anabaptists than with Luther or Calvin.

A Call to Truth

This book is not an attack on evangelicalism but a critical reflection on its trajectory. I affirm evangelicals as part of the Christian family, yet I believe truth demands scrutiny. The Reformation was a quest for truth—Scripture-grounded, community-shaped, and worship-disciplined. Bonhoeffer's critique of "cheap grace" in *The Cost of Discipleship* (1937) sharpens this lens: he decried a faith without sacrifice or accountability, a charge that rings true in much of today's evangelicalism, where personal fulfillment often overshadows gospel demands.

We'll also examine evangelicalism's radical fringes—like modern polygamist sects justifying their practices with literalist readings, echoing the Anabaptists of Münster—to highlight the risks of unchecked individualism. These extremes, while not typical, expose the absence of confessional guardrails, a concern Bonhoeffer shared.

The Road Ahead

In the chapters that follow, we'll explore:

- The Reformation's communal, confessional vision (Chapter 1).

- Early radicals like the Paulicians and Bogomils as departures from orthodoxy (Chapter 2).

- Evangelicalism's drift toward individualism in Pentecostal and nondenominational forms (Chapter 3).

- Radical evangelical fringes as symptoms of this shift (Chapter 4).

Why Many Evangelicals are Not Protestant: The Creedless Drift

- Evangelicalism's cultural conformity versus the Reformation's countercultural witness (Chapter 5).

- Whether evangelicalism can reclaim its Protestant roots—or if it's become something new (Chapter 6).

What would Luther, Calvin, and Bonhoeffer say about a modern evangelical service? Would they see their legacy—or a radical echo of the movements they opposed? This book invites you to wrestle with that question and ponder evangelicalism's future in light of its past.

Virgil A. Walker

Chapter 1: The Reformation's Communal, Confessional Vision

What does it mean to be a Christian church? For the first fifteen centuries of Christianity, the answer was clear: a community bound by shared creeds, sacramental worship, and ecclesiastical authority, united in confessing Christ as Lord. The Protestant Reformation of the 16th century, far from dismantling this vision, sought to purify it, grounding the church in *sola scriptura* (Scripture alone), *sola fide* (faith alone), and a disciplined communal life. Yet today, much of modern evangelicalism—particularly its Pentecostal and nondenominational strands—has drifted from this foundation, embracing an individualism that reformers like Martin Luther, John Calvin, and Thomas Cranmer, as well as later voices like Dietrich Bonhoeffer, would have found alien. To understand evangelicalism's radical departure, we must first grasp the historic Christian and Reformation ideals it has left behind. This chapter defines those ideals, setting the stage for their contrast with evangelicalism's Anabaptist-like tendencies.

The Pillars of Historic Christianity

Historic Christianity, from the early church through the Middle Ages, rested on three pillars: creeds, sacraments, and ecclesiology. These were not mere traditions but communal commitments, ensuring the church's unity and fidelity to Christ's gospel. The Reformation refined these pillars, preserving their role as anchors of faith against radical dissent.

Creeds: Affirming Communal Orthodoxy

Creeds were the church's heartbeat, articulating shared belief in a world rife with division. The Apostles' Creed, emerging in the 2nd century, summarized core Christian doctrines: the Trinity, Christ's incarnation, death, resurrection, and return. Used in catechesis and baptism, it unified believers in confessing "I believe in God the Father Almighty, Maker of heaven and earth." The Nicene Creed, crafted at the Council of Nicaea (325 AD) and revised at Constantinople (381 AD), clarified Christ's divinity, declaring Him "of one substance" (*homoousios*) with the Father, co-equal and eternal. Recited in worship, these creeds were not individual opinions but communal affirmations, binding the church across time and space.

Creeds arose to combat heresies that threatened Christian unity. In the 2nd–3rd centuries, Gnosticism denied

Christ's humanity and creation's goodness, teaching salvation through secret knowledge. The Apostles' Creed countered this, affirming Christ's birth, suffering, and bodily resurrection. Docetism, claiming Christ only appeared human, was refuted by the creed's insistence on His real incarnation. In the 4th century, Arianism, led by Arius of Alexandria, taught Christ was a created being, subordinate to the Father. The Nicene Council, convened by Emperor Constantine, rejected Arianism, with Athanasius defending Christ's divinity. The Nicene Creed's *homoousios* clause was a bulwark against Arian error, ensuring orthodoxy. Sabellianism, denying the Trinity's distinct persons, further necessitated creedal clarity, affirming "one God in three Persons."

These councils were not academic exercises but urgent responses to division. As Jaroslav Pelikan notes in *Heresies and How to Combat Them* (1957), creeds "defined the boundaries of faith, guarding the church against speculative individualism." They shaped worship as a collective act, recited to affirm shared confession, a practice the Reformation upheld. Luther's *Large Catechism* (1529) taught the Apostles' Creed as "the sum of Christian doctrine," while Calvin's *Institutes* (1536) grounded theology in Nicene orthodoxy. This creedal commitment contrasts sharply with Anabaptist rejection of creeds as human traditions and evangelicalism's "no creed but the Bible" ethos, a departure reformers would condemn.

Sacraments: Signs of Communal Grace

The sacraments—baptism and the Eucharist—were tangible signs of God's grace, binding the church as a covenantal body. Baptism welcomed members into the community, marking their incorporation into Christ's body. The Eucharist nourished believers' union with Christ and one another, a communal act of remembrance and renewal. Early church fathers like Augustine saw sacraments as "visible words," uniting the church in God's promises.

The Reformation refined sacramental theology. Luther's *Large Catechism* upheld baptism and communion as means of grace, while Calvin's *Institutes* called them "seals" of God's covenant. Cranmer's *Book of Common Prayer* (1549) embedded sacraments in liturgy, ensuring communal participation. These sacraments were not private rituals but corporate acts, a standard evangelicalism's casual approach often neglects.

Ecclesiology: The Church's Communal Structure

Ecclesiology ensured the church's accountability. Bishops, councils, and later Protestant consistories guided doctrine and discipline, preventing individualistic error. The

Reformation preserved this structure, with Luther's congregationalism, Calvin's consistory, and Cranmer's episcopal framework. Bonhoeffer's *Sanctorum Communio* (1927) echoed this, defining the church as "Christ existing as community." This communal ecclesiology clashed with Anabaptist congregational autonomy and evangelicalism's nondenominational independence.

Luther's Congregationalism: The Church as Community

Martin Luther's church was a community bound by Word and sacrament. His doctrine of the priesthood of all believers empowered every Christian to proclaim the gospel within the church's structure, not as isolated individuals. In *The German Mass* (1526), Luther retained hymns, prayers, and the Lord's Supper for congregational participation. His Eucharistic theology, articulated in *The Babylonian Captivity of the Church* (1520), rejected Catholic transubstantiation but affirmed Christ's real presence "in, with, and under" the bread and wine—a *sacramental union* uniting the congregation in receiving God's promise. His *Small Catechism* (1529) taught believers to approach communion with faith and repentance, reinforcing its communal role: "It is given as a daily nourishment and sustenance to the church."

Why Many Evangelicals are Not Protestant: The Creedless Drift

Luther's commitment to infant baptism further underscored community. In *The Large Catechism*, he argued baptism incorporates children into God's covenant, not as an individual act but a communal pledge. This clashed with Anabaptists, whom Luther condemned in *Against the Heavenly Prophets* (1525) for rejecting infant baptism and viewing sacraments as mere symbols. He called their individualism "schismatic," accusing them of undermining the church's sacramental unity. Luther's congregationalism, disciplined by pastors and creeds like the Augsburg Confession (1530), would view evangelicalism's casual communion and nondenominational autonomy as a betrayal of historic Christianity.

Calvin's Disciplined Geneva: Order and Covenant

John Calvin's Geneva embodied a systematic, sacramental vision. In *Institutes* (Book IV), he defined the church by "the Word of God purely preached and heard, and the sacraments administered according to Christ's institution." Sacraments were "seals" of God's promises, uniting believers to Christ through the Spirit. Baptism, he argued in *Geneva Catechism* (1541), incorporates infants into the covenant community, signifying God's initiative, not human choice. The Eucharist offered Christ's spiritual presence, nourishing faith through communal participation, with strict preparation ensuring reverence.

Calvin's *Ecclesiastical Ordinances* (1541) structured worship to emphasize Word and sacrament, rejecting emotional excess. His critique of Anabaptists in *Treatise Against the Anabaptists* (1544) was sharp: their rejection of infant baptism and symbolic view of communion "tear apart the church's covenant." Calvin's sacramental theology, rooted in communal order, would condemn evangelicalism's informal baptisms (e.g., megachurch events) and Pentecostal spontaneity as un-historic, echoing Anabaptist chaos.

Cranmer's Liturgical Reform: Unity in Worship

Thomas Cranmer shaped the Church of England through the *Book of Common Prayer* (1549), embedding sacraments in communal worship. His liturgical prayers for baptism and Eucharist emphasized corporate participation, uniting believers in Christ's body. In *Defence of the True and Catholic Doctrine of the Sacrament* (1550), Cranmer rejected transubstantiation but affirmed a spiritual presence, balancing Luther's real presence and Calvin's spiritual union. Baptism welcomed infants into the church's covenant, while communion strengthened communal faith. Cranmer's *Homilies* (1547) reinforced sacramental doctrine, countering radical tendencies among English reformers.

Cranmer's structured liturgy stood against Anabaptist informality, which dismissed sacraments as secondary. His vision would clash with evangelicalism's freeform services, where communion is often an afterthought and baptism a personal milestone, lacking Reformation reverence.

Bonhoeffer's Communal Vision: A Modern Echo

Dietrich Bonhoeffer, a 20th-century Lutheran, reaffirmed the Reformation's sacramental community in *Sanctorum Communio* (1927). He saw the church as "Christ existing as community," where sacraments bind believers in mutual accountability. Baptism incorporates individuals into the body, while communion, per *Life Together* (1939), is a shared confession of dependence on Christ's grace: "In the Lord's Supper, we receive Christ together, not alone." Bonhoeffer's *The Cost of Discipleship* (1937) rejected "cheap grace"—salvation without discipline—implicitly critiquing individualistic sacramental neglect.

Bonhoeffer's vision echoed Luther's congregationalism and Calvin's covenantal order, opposing the subjective spirituality of his day. He would likely see evangelicalism's solo spirituality—nondenominational minimalism or

Pentecostal emotionalism—as a radical departure, lacking the sacramental fellowship of historic Christianity.

The Anabaptist Contrast: A Radical Departure

The Anabaptists, emerging in the 1520s, challenged the Reformation's vision of historic Christianity, revealing a radical individualism that reformers like Luther, Calvin, and Cranmer would see echoed in modern evangelicalism. Yet their diversity cautions against overgeneralization. While unified in rejecting infant baptism and ecclesiastical hierarchy, Anabaptist groups varied widely: pacifist Mennonites, following Menno Simons' nonviolent ethic, formed separatist communities; communal Hutterites shared possessions in isolated colonies; and the radical Münsterites (1534–1535) pursued apocalypticism and polygamy, shocking even fellow Anabaptists. Despite this spectrum, their shared emphasis on personal faith over institutional authority clashed with the Reformation's communal standard.

Anabaptist practices offer specific parallels to evangelical individualism. Leaders like Balthasar Hubmaier, in *On the Christian Baptism of Believers* (1525), rejected infant baptism as unbiblical, insisting on believer's baptism as a personal act of faith, sidelining the covenantal community Luther and Calvin upheld. Similarly, Menno Simons' *Foundation of*

Why Many Evangelicals are Not Protestant: The Creedless Drift

Christian Doctrine (1539) viewed the Eucharist as a memorial, not a means of communal grace, echoing the subjective spirituality of early dissenters. These practices mirror modern evangelicalism's Pentecostal emphasis on personal spiritual gifts, such as speaking in tongues or prophetic utterances, which prioritize direct revelation over creedal or sacramental authority. Nondenominational evangelicalism's "no creed but the Bible" ethos further aligns with Anabaptist rejection of human traditions, favoring individual interpretation over communal confession.

Yet differences abound. Many Anabaptists, like Mennonites, sought communal purity through separation from the world, forming tight-knit communities governed by shared discipline. In contrast, evangelical megachurches embrace cultural consumerism, adopting market-driven models like Hillsong's branded worship or seeker-sensitive sermons. Despite these distinctions, both sideline Reformation structures—creeds, sacraments, and ecclesiology—favoring a faith rooted in personal experience, a radical departure the reformers condemned.

Luther, in *Against the Heavenly Prophets* (1525), accused Anabaptists of "enthusiasm"—a subjective faith undermining Scripture's authority within the church's communal framework. Calvin, in *Treatise Against the*

Virgil A. Walker

Anabaptists (1544), called their rejection of infant baptism and symbolic sacraments "fanatical," arguing they fractured the church's covenantal unity. The Münster rebellion, with its polygamy and apocalyptic fervor, epitomized this chaos, horrifying reformers as a betrayal of historic Christianity's order.

The Reformers' Lens: Judging Evangelicalism

The reformers' standard for the church was clear: fidelity to Scripture, expressed through communal worship, confessional clarity, and ecclesiastical discipline. They judged movements by their adherence to these marks, condemning Anabaptists for their subjective, structureless faith. Applying this lens to modern evangelicalism reveals a stark contrast. The megachurch's consumerist worship, the Pentecostal focus on personal revelation, and the nondenominational disdain for creeds would dismay Luther, who valued congregational unity, Calvin, who demanded order, and Cranmer, who crafted communal liturgy. Bonhoeffer, warning against "cheap grace," would see evangelicalism's individualism as a betrayal of the church as *sanctorum communio*.

This chapter has outlined the historic Christian and Reformation vision: a church defined by creeds, sacraments, and structure, not individual experience. As we turn to early radicals like the Paulicians and Bogomils, we'll see how their departures from this vision set a precedent for Anabaptist and evangelical radicalism, viewed through the reformers' critical lens.

Sources

- **Bonhoeffer, Dietrich.** *Life Together.* 1939.
- **Bonhoeffer, Dietrich.** *Sanctorum Communio.* 1927.
- **Calvin, John.** *Geneva Catechism.* 1541.
- **Calvin, John.** *Institutes of the Christian Religion.* 1536.
- **Cranmer, Thomas.** *Book of Common Prayer.* 1549.
- **Cranmer, Thomas.** *Defence of the True and Catholic Doctrine of the Sacrament.* 1550.
- **Davis, Leo Donald.** The First Seven Ecumenical Councils. 1983.
- **Hubmaier, Balthasar.** *On the Christian Baptism of Believers.* 1525.
- **Jurgens, William A.** The Faith of the Early Fathers. 1970.

- Kelly, J.N.D. *Early Christian Creeds*. 1972.
- Luther, Martin. *Against the Heavenly Prophets*. 1525.
- Luther, Martin. *The Babylonian Captivity of the Church*. 1520.
- Luther, Martin. *Small Catechism*. 1529.
- Pelikan, Jaroslav. *Heresies and How to Combat Them*. 1957.
- Schaff, Philip. *The Creeds Of Christendom*. 1877.
- Simons, Menno. *Foundation of Christian Doctrine*. 1539.
- Williams, George Huntston. *The Radical Reformation*. 1992.

Chapter 2: Early Radicals: Paulicians, Bogomils, and the Seeds of Dissent

The Protestant Reformation sought to restore historic Christianity's communal, confessional core, but it was not the first challenge to ecclesiastical orthodoxy. Centuries earlier, radical movements like the Paulicians (7th–9th centuries), Bogomils (10th–15th centuries), and Cathars (12th–13th centuries) rejected the church's hierarchy, sacraments, and creedal traditions, embracing individualistic and often dualistic faith. These dissenters, while not direct ancestors of the Anabaptists or modern evangelicalism, sowed seeds of radicalism that prefigure the autonomy and biblicism of later movements. Some evangelicals, following E.H. Broadbent's *The Pilgrim Church* (1931), view these groups as protectors of "true Christianity," dismissing accusations of heresy as false—a perspective aligning with evangelical individualism but diverging from the reformers' communal vision. For Martin Luther, and John Calvin such departures from historic Christianity's creeds, sacraments, and ecclesiology were heretical, a lens that would condemn evangelicalism's Pentecostal and nondenominational tendencies as un-

Protestant. This chapter explores these early radicals, loosely tied to Anabaptist and evangelical individualism, while unequivocally condemning their brutal persecution as morally wrong.

The Danger of Heresy: Gnosticism as a Precedent

To contextualize Paulician, Bogomil, and Cathar radicalism, we consider earlier heresies like Gnosticism, which shaped the church's creedal defenses. Emerging in the 2nd–3rd centuries, Gnostic sects taught salvation through secret knowledge (*gnosis*), rejecting material creation and Christ's incarnation as illusory (Docetism). Texts like the *Gospel of Thomas* (c. 150 AD) prioritized esoteric spirituality over communal orthodoxy, prompting the Apostles' Creed to affirm Christ's bodily incarnation and resurrection. As Jaroslav Pelikan notes in *Heresies and How to Combat Them* (1957), Gnostic individualism "undermined the church's unity," necessitating creedal clarity. While Gnostics share no direct link with Anabaptists or evangelicals, their subjective faith and rejection of ecclesiastical authority set a precedent for later dissenters, who prioritized personal piety over institutional norms. Luther and Calvin, steeped in creedal orthodoxy, would see such movements as threats to the church's communal fabric, a critique extending to evangelicalism's solo spirituality.

The Paulicians: Rejecting Byzantine Orthodoxy

In 7th-century Armenia, the Paulicians, led by Constantine of Mananalis (adopting the name Silvanus, after Paul's companion), challenged Byzantine Christianity's formalism. Petrus of Sicily's *History of the Paulicians* (c. 870) describes their rejection of the church's hierarchy, sacraments, and veneration of the cross, stating, "They dishonor the precious cross, calling it mere wood, and reject the holy mysteries [sacraments]." Theophanes the Confessor (c. 800 AD) labels them dualists, claiming an evil Demiurge ruled this world, while Gregory Magistros (d. 1058) notes their Adoptionist view, linking them to Paul of Samosata's teaching that Jesus was human, not divine. Islamic polemicist al-Jāḥiẓ (d. 868) critiques their anti-institutionalism in *Kitāb al-Ḥayawān*, noting their influence on Muslim debates about Christian disunity. Abū ʿĪsā al-Warrāq (d. 861) cites their rejection of Trinitarian orthodoxy in *Against the Trinity*.

These sources—primarily Byzantine and Islamic polemics—are one-sided, often exaggerating heresy to justify persecution. *The Key of Truth* (discovered 1837, per

Conybeare, 1898) suggests a Christian framework, accepting symbolic baptism and Eucharist, but its late 18th-century manuscript may reflect Tondrakian or Protestant influence, not all Paulicians, much like Anabaptist diversity (Mennonites vs. Münsterites). Carl Dixon's *The Paulicians* (2022) cautions that Petrus and Theophanes reflect Orthodox bias. Some evangelicals, per E.H. Broadbent's *The Pilgrim Church* (1931), view Paulicians as proto-Protestants preserving apostolic faith, dismissing dualism charges as slander, a defense echoing evangelical skepticism of institutional authority.

Paulician factionalism adds nuance: Baanites, under Baanes (c. 837), were militaristic, leading rebellions, while Sergijites, under Sergius-Tychicus (c. 801–835), focused on doctrinal reform, per Nina Garsoïan's *The Paulician Heresy* (1967). Relocated to Thrace (747, 970) as frontier forces, Paulicians faced brutal persecution—Constantine-Silvanus was stoned (668), Simeon-Titus burned (c. 690)—acts of murder and torture we unequivocally condemn as morally wrong, without endorsing their beliefs. Their rejection of sacraments and hierarchy, rooted in a biblicist focus on Paul's epistles, mirrors the "just me and my Bible" ethos of modern nondenominationalism. Would Thomas Cranmer, whose *Book of Common Prayer* (1549) embedded sacraments in communal worship, see in Paulician individualism a precursor to evangelical casual communion? Baptist historian John T. Christian, in *A History of the Baptists* (1922), suggests such biblicism influenced Anabaptist autonomy, a tendency that risks fracturing the unity Christ prayed for in John 17:20–23, where He called His followers to be "one" as He and the Father are one.

The Bogomils: Dualistic Piety in the Balkans

Influenced by Paulicians relocated to Thrace, the Bogomils emerged in 10th-century Bulgaria under the priest Bogomil. Dmitri Obolensky's *The Bogomils* (1948) details their rejection of Orthodox clergy, sacraments, and church buildings, viewing the body as the temple and practicing fasting or ritual dances for spiritual purity. Cosmas the Priest's *Against the Newly-Appeared Heresy of the Bogomils* (c. 970) describes their moderate dualism—God ruling the spiritual, Satan the material as God's inferior son. Orthodox sources, like Cosmas, exaggerate heresy to justify crusades, which included torture and execution, acts we condemn as morally reprehensible. Muslim polemicist al-Warrāq noted their anti-institutionalism, using it to critique Christian disunity.

Some evangelicals, following E.H. Broadbent's *The Pilgrim Church* (1931), defend Bogomils as preservers of pure faith, arguing accusations of dualism were fabricated by corrupt clergy. This apologetic aligns with evangelical rejection of institutional traditions, mirroring Bogomil anti-hierarchy. Their influence spread to Serbia, Kievan Rus', and Italy, shaping Cathars, per Obolensky. Yet their emphasis on subjective spirituality over communal structures raises a question: would the Reformers see in Bogomil piety a precursor to nondenominational autonomy? Philipp Melanchthon, in the *Augsburg Confession* (1530), emphasized the church as a "congregation of saints" bound by Word and sacrament, a standard that would reject Bogomil rejection of clergy and rituals as schismatic. Modern evangelical scholars like D.A. Carson, in *The Gagging of God* (1996), warn that unchecked individualism risks diluting biblical community, a concern that echoes the Bogomils' legacy in today's creedless worship.

The Cathars: Dualistic Dissent in the West

The Cathars, flourishing in 12th–13th-century Southern France, marked a high point of medieval dualistic dissent. Influenced by Bogomils via Balkan missionaries, they rejected Catholic hierarchy, sacraments, and creeds, teaching absolute dualism—two opposing gods, one spiritual, one material. Sean Martin's *The Cathars* (2004) describes their *Consolamentum*, a spiritual baptism for the elite "Perfect," replacing water baptism, and their rejection of the Eucharist, viewing material elements as corrupt. Yuri Stoyanov's *The Other God* (2000) notes their biblicism, emphasizing New Testament teachings, akin to Paulician focus on Paul's epistles. Cathars formed autonomous communities, often supported by local nobles, until the Albigensian Crusade (1209–1229) crushed them with mass burnings and executions—acts of murder and torture we unequivocally condemn as morally wrong, without endorsing their beliefs.

Some modern groups, per Broadbent's *The Pilgrim Church*, romanticize Cathars as defenders of pure Christianity, dismissing dualism charges as Catholic propaganda. This mirrors evangelical skepticism of institutional authority, aligning with nondenominational rejection of creeds. Luther's creedal fidelity (*Large Catechism*, 1529) would condemn Cathar biblicism as schismatic, while Calvin's *Institutes* would reject their dualism as heretical, a critique extending to evangelicalism's solo spirituality.

Modern Apologetics for Early Radicals

The modern evangelical defense of Paulicians, Bogomils, and Cathars, exemplified by Broadbent's *The Pilgrim Church*, reveals a shared radical ethos. Broadbent argues these groups preserved apostolic Christianity, claiming, "The Paulicians, Bogomils, and Cathars held fast to the Scriptures, rejecting false traditions of corrupt churches."

This view, echoed in Baptist and nondenominational circles (*Anabaptist Perspectives*, 2020), dismisses accusations of dualism or Adoptionism as slander, paralleling evangelical skepticism of creeds and denominational authority. Such apologetics reflect the "no creed but the Bible" mindset, akin to Anabaptist biblicism, which Luther and Calvin would see as un-Protestant. While we condemn the murder and torture of these dissenters, their individualistic rejection of historic Christianity's communal framework aligns with evangelical tendencies, setting the stage for later radicalism.

Loose Connections to Anabaptists and Evangelicals

Paulician, Bogomil, and Cathar anti-hierarchy and biblicism loosely prefigure Anabaptist autonomy and evangelical individualism, though doctrinal differences (e.g., dualism) limit direct links. Paulician focus on Paul's epistles and Cathar emphasis on New Testament purity mirror Anabaptist reliance on the Sermon on the Mount (e.g., Hubmaier's *On the Christian Baptism of Believers*, 1525). Bogomil rejection of clergy echoes Anabaptist congregationalism and Pentecostal emphasis on direct revelation (e.g., tongues). Yet their dualism contrasts with Anabaptist orthodoxy, and their separatist piety differs from evangelical cultural engagement (e.g., megachurch consumerism). John T. Christian's *A History of the Baptists* (1922) suggests Bogomil ideas "lurked underground," possibly influencing Anabaptist autonomy, but evidence is speculative.

Reformers would see these movements as radical departures. Luther's creedal fidelity would condemn Paulician and Cathar biblicism as schismatic, akin to Anabaptist error. Calvin would reject Bogomil and Cathar dualism as heretical, extending this to evangelicalism's nondenominational spirituality. Bonhoeffer's communal vision in *Life Together* would view all three as undermining the church, a lens framing evangelicalism's solo faith as un-Protestant.

The Reformers' Verdict: Radicalism as Betrayal

For Luther, Calvin, and Cranmer the church was a communal body defined by creeds, sacraments, and structure. Paulician, Bogomil, and Cathar individualism—rejecting hierarchy, sacraments, and creedal orthodoxy—would be anathema, prefiguring Anabaptist autonomy and evangelicalism's Pentecostal/nondenominational tendencies. Modern evangelical apologetics, while rightly condemning their persecution, romanticize their radicalism, aligning with evangelical individualism. As we turn to evangelicalism's theological drift, we'll see how these early seeds of dissent bear fruit in practices the reformers would condemn.

Sources

- Bonhoeffer, Dietrich. *Life Together.* 1939.
- Broadbent, E.H. *The Pilgrim Church.* 1931.
- Calvin, John. *Institutes of the Christian Religion.* 1536.
- Calvin, John. *Treatise Against the Anabaptists.* 1544.
- Christian, John T. *A History of the Baptists.* 1922.
- Conybeare, Frederick C. *The Key of Truth.* 1898.
- Dixon, Carl. *The Paulicians: Heresy, Persecution and Warfare on the Byzantine Frontier, c.750–880.* 2022.
- Garsoïan, Nina. *The Paulician Heresy.* 1967.
- Hubmaier, Balthasar. *On the Christian Baptism of Believers.* 1525.
- Jāḥiẓ, al-. *Kitāb al-Ḥayawān.* 1991.
- Kelly, J.N.D. *Early Christian Creeds.* 1972.

- Luther, Martin. *Against the Heavenly Prophets*. 1525.

- Martin, Sean. *The Cathars: The Most Successful Heresy of the Middle Ages*. 2004.

- Obolensky, Dmitri. *The Bogomils: A Study in Balkan Neo-Manichaeism*. 1948.

- Pelikan, Jaroslav. *Heresies and How to Combat Them*. 1957.

- Peter of Sicily. *History of the Paulicians*. c. 870.

- Stoyanov, Yuri. *The Other God: Dualist Religions from Antiquity to the Cathar Heresy*. 2000.

- Warrāq, Abū ʿĪsā al-. *Against the Trinity*. 1992.

- Williams, George Huntston. *The Radical Reformation*. 1992.

Virgil A. Walker

Chapter 3: Theological Drift: From Sola Scriptura to Solo Spirituality

The Protestant Reformation anchored the church in *sola scriptura*—Scripture as the supreme authority, interpreted within a communal, confessional framework. Martin Luther, and John Calvin upheld doctrinal rigor, emphasizing justification by faith and the church as a covenantal body. Despite internal debates, such as Luther versus Zwingli on the Eucharist, Lutheranism's conservative Reformation and Anglicanism's *via media* preserved creeds and essentials for unity. Yet modern evangelicalism, particularly its Pentecostal, nondenominational, and Southern Baptist strands, has drifted from this vision, prioritizing experiential faith and personal revelation over Reformation orthodoxy. Enabled by materialistic and celebrity pastor culture, fostering heresies like the prosperity gospel and Oneness Pentecostalism, this shift echoes the individualism of Paulicians, Bogomils, Cathars, and Anabaptists—though Anabaptists maintained stronger communalism. This drift would be unrecognizable to the reformers as Protestant. Luther would call Pentecostal fervor "fanaticism," akin to

Why Many Evangelicals are Not Protestant: The Creedless Drift

Anabaptist chaos; Calvin would condemn nondenominational laxity as a betrayal of the covenant. Bonhoeffer's critique of "cheap grace" in *The Cost of Discipleship* (1937) sharpens this lens, exposing evangelicalism's solo spirituality as a radical departure from historic Christianity. This chapter explores this drift, addressing evangelical defenses and contrasting confessional Reformed Baptists with radical evangelical tendencies

The Reformers' Doctrinal Rigor: Justification and Communal Faith

The Reformation's cornerstone was justification by faith alone (*sola fide*), grounded in *sola scriptura*. Luther's *The Freedom of a Christian* (1520) taught that faith in Christ's atoning work justifies the believer, uniting them to the church's communal confession. His *sola scriptura*, per *The Bondage of the Will* (1525), meant Scripture's authority within the church's framework—guided by creeds like the Augsburg Confession (1530) and interpreted by clergy. Alister McGrath's *Reformation Thought* (2012) notes Lutheranism's "conservative" approach, preserving sacraments and creeds against radical Anabaptists, unlike the *solo scriptura* of modern evangelicals, where individual interpretation trumps tradition.

Virgil A. Walker

Calvin, in *Institutes of the Christian Religion* (1536), defined justification as "the acceptance with which God receives us into his favor," received through Word and sacrament. His *sola scriptura* demanded communal exegesis, rooted in Nicene orthodoxy. Cranmer's Anglican *via media*, per *Book of Common Prayer* (1549), balanced Catholic tradition and Protestant reform, embedding justification and creeds (Nicene, Apostles') in liturgy for unity, as Richard Hooker's *Of the Laws of Ecclesiastical Polity* (1593) defends: "Scripture is supreme, yet interpreted by reason and tradition." Bonhoeffer's *Sanctorum Communio* (1927) echoed this, seeing the church as "Christ existing as community," bound by doctrine.

This rigor contrasted with earlier radicals. Paulicians prioritized Paul's epistles over creeds, Bogomils rejected sacraments, and Cathars emphasized spiritual purity. Anabaptists, from pacifist Mennonites to radical Münsterites, favored personal conversion over communal doctrine. Luther's *Against the Heavenly Prophets* (1525) condemned this as "enthusiasm," undermining Scripture's communal authority. Calvin's *Treatise Against the Anabaptists* (1544) called their theology "fanatical," fracturing the covenant. The reformers' *sola scriptura*—communal, creedal, disciplined—sets a standard evangelicalism often fails.

Why Many Evangelicals are Not Protestant: The Creedless Drift

The Erosion of Christology: Survey Evidence of Creedless Drift

One of the most alarming manifestations of evangelicalism's theological individualism is the erosion of orthodox Christology, a cornerstone of historic Christianity affirmed in the Nicene Creed (325 AD), which declares Christ "of one substance with the Father." Without creedal safeguards to anchor biblical interpretation, *solo scriptura* opens the door to heresies that deny Christ's divinity, echoing early radical movements like Gnosticism and Arianism (Chapter 2). A 2022 survey by Ligonier Ministries and LifeWay Research revealed that 43% of U.S. evangelicals agreed that "Jesus was a great teacher, but he was not God," up from 30% in 2020 (Ligonier Ministries and LifeWay Research 2022). This shift, representing over two in five evangelicals, indicates a significant departure from Reformation orthodoxy, where Luther's *Large Catechism* (1529) and Calvin's *Institutes of the Christian Religion* (1536) upheld Christ's deity as essential to justification by faith.

The survey's findings underscore the dangers of unchecked personal revelation, prevalent in Pentecostal emphasis on spiritual gifts and nondenominational biblicism. When Scripture is interpreted without the communal guardrails of creeds, as in the Anglican Church in North America's *To Be a Christian* (2014), it leads to subjective views that undermine the Church's unity (Galatians 3:28–29). Bonhoeffer's *The Cost of Discipleship* (1937) warns against "cheap grace," a critique applicable to this Christological drift: denying Christ's divinity reduces him to a moral example, not the divine Savior. Luther would call this "fanaticism," akin to Anabaptist chaos (*Against the Heavenly Prophets*, 1525), while Calvin's *Treatise Against the Anabaptists* (1544) condemned similar errors as fracturing the covenant. Without creeds to affirm Christ's co-equality with the Father, evangelicalism risks reviving ancient heresies, proving that when safeguards are absent, theological erosion follows.

The Mormon Parallel: A Case of Unchecked Individualism

The perils of theological individualism extend beyond evangelicalism, as evidenced by The Church of Jesus Christ of Latter-day Saints, founded in 1830 by Joseph Smith. This movement exemplifies how *solo scriptura* fosters drift when creedal safeguards are absent. Smith claimed a series of visions beginning in 1820, when Heavenly Father and Jesus Christ appeared to him, instructing him not to join any existing churches due to their "incorrect doctrines." Later visions included the angel Moroni in 1823, revealing golden plates containing

Why Many Evangelicals are Not Protestant: The Creedless Drift

the Book of Mormon, which Smith translated and published in 1830. Smith positioned himself as a prophet, restoring the "true" gospel, including priesthood authority, temple work, and additional scriptures.

However, Smith's claims have faced scrutiny for their sketchy nature. Multiple versions of the First Vision story exist, with varying details, and critics highlight imprecise dates and alleged false prophecies, such as Smith's 1843 prediction that he could not be killed within five years, contradicted by his death in 1844. The Book of Mormon lacks archaeological support, with no evidence for its claimed ancient American civilizations, despite Smith's assertions. These issues suggest a reliance on personal revelation without historical or scriptural corroboration.

Official Mormon statements emphasize accepting Smith's claims on faith, regardless of evidence. The church teaches that a testimony comes from studying the Book of Mormon and praying for confirmation through the Holy Ghost, promising manifestation of truth if sought with "real intent" (churchofjesuschrist.org). This approach, while faith-based, bypasses creedal orthodoxy like the Nicene Creed's affirmation of Christ's divinity, leading to non-Trinitarian views (a corporeal God and multiple deities). Historical practices like polygamy, discontinued in 1890, further diverge from Reformation orthodoxy. This parallel underscores how, absent creedal safeguards, theological drift produces heresies, a lesson for evangelicals navigating their own *solo scriptura* path (GotQuestions.org; churchofjesuschrist.org).

The Jehovah's Witness Divergence: Misnaming God and Rejecting the Trinity

Theological individualism's reach extends to Jehovah's Witnesses, founded in 1870 by Charles Taze Russell, further illustrating *solo scriptura*'s drift. Rejecting the Nicene and Apostles' Creeds, they deny Christ's divinity, viewing Jesus as a created being subordinate to Jehovah, echoing Arianism (Kelly, *Early Christian Creeds*, 1972). Their use of "Jehovah" as God's name, popularized from a 13th-century mispronunciation of the Hebrew "YHWH" (likely "Yahweh"), reflects historical inaccuracy, as "Ja" lacks Hebrew basis. Evangelicals and similar groups sometimes adopt this term in songs and flags, unaware of its distortion, a trend fueled by *solo scriptura*'s neglect of creedal scholarship.

Russell's claims of prophetic insight, including failed 1914 end-times predictions, and the Watchtower Society's control over doctrine raise questions of legitimacy. Official statements demand faith in these teachings despite lacking historical or archaeological evidence, mirroring Mormon reliance on personal revelation

Why Many Evangelicals are Not Protestant: The Creedless Drift

(GotQuestions.org; jw.org). This divergence, absent Trinitarian orthodoxy, underscores how unguided interpretation breeds heresy, a caution for evangelicals facing their own creedal erosion.

Pentecostal Fervor: Personal Revelation Over Doctrine

Pentecostalism, sparked by the Azusa Street Revival (1906), marks a profound evangelical departure, prioritizing spiritual gifts—tongues, prophecy, healing—over Reformation rigor. Vinson Synan's *The Global Pentecostal Movement* (2017) notes that Pentecostalism, encompassing ~20% of U.S. evangelicals (Pew Research, 2020), emphasizes direct revelation, with believers seeking divine messages through ecstatic experiences. This mirrors Anabaptist conversionism, as in Balthasar Hubmaier's believer's baptism (*On the Christian Baptism of Believers*, 1525), prioritizing subjective experience over institutional authority. Paul's instructions in 1 Corinthians 14:27–28—"If anyone speaks in a tongue, let there be two or at the most three, each in turn, and let one interpret. But if there is no interpreter, let him keep silent in church"—are often ignored in Pentecostal services, where unverified tongues dominate, reflecting a lack of scriptural discipline akin to Paulician biblicism.

A Pentecostal healing service—worshipers, swayed by emotive music, seeking miraculous cures guided by prophetic words—contrasts with Calvin's expository preaching in Geneva, unpacking Scripture for doctrinal clarity. Calvin would denounce this emotionalism as "fanatical," per his *Treatise*. Bonhoeffer's *The Cost of Discipleship* critiques such fervor as "cheap grace"—"preaching forgiveness without requiring repentance"—lacking costly discipleship. Luther's *sola scriptura*, rooted in communal exegesis, would reject Pentecostal reliance on personal revelation as un-Protestant, echoing Anabaptist chaos.

Nondenominationalism and Southern Baptists: Biblical Simplicity as Solo Spirituality

Nondenominational churches, the fastest-growing evangelical segment (Hartford Institute, 2021), amplify this drift by rejecting creeds for "biblical" simplicity. David F. Wells' *The Courage to Be Protestant* (2008) argues their "no creed but the Bible" ethos fosters *solo scriptura*, where individual interpretation trumps communal confession. Celebrity pastors like Steven Furtick deliver sermons on personal fulfillment—e.g., "God's plan for your life"—sidelining justification or covenantal theology, often in megachurches with consumerist aesthetics

Why Many Evangelicals are Not Protestant: The Creedless Drift

(*Christianity Today*, 2022). This mirrors Paulician focus on Paul's epistles and Anabaptist rejection of creeds, as Menno Simons' *Foundation of Christian Doctrine* (1539) prioritized Scripture alone.

The Southern Baptist Convention (SBC), per *Baptist Faith and Message* (2000), similarly prioritizes Scripture over historic creeds, embracing *solo scriptura*. Albert Mohler's *The Baptist Story* (2015) notes their emphasis on personal conversion and eternal security ("once saved, always saved"), which can foster theological laxity, overlapping with prosperity gospel's assurance. Unlike Reformed Baptists, who adhere to the 1689 London Baptist Confession and historic creeds, affirming Amillennialism (e.g., John Piper), the SBC often embraces Dispensationalism, a 19th-century innovation by John Darby, per Charles Ryrie's *Dispensationalism* (1995). Dispensationalism's premillennialism and rapture theology contrast with Reformation Amillennialism, aligning with Pentecostal/nondenominational radicalism. Reformed Baptists' confessional fidelity, rooted in Nicene orthodoxy, reflects historic Christianity, unlike SBC's biblicism.

Nondenominational and SBC services, with casual worship and seeker-sensitive approaches, contrast with Cranmer's *via media*, where creeds unified believers.

Hooker's *Ecclesiastical Polity* defends this: "The church's tradition guards Scripture's truth." Luther's *Large Catechism* would view their biblicism as schismatic. Bonhoeffer's "cheap grace" critique applies: their laxity, driven by materialism and celebrity culture, undermines the church as *sanctorum communio*.

Heresies Enabled by Individualism: Prosperity Gospel and Oneness Pentecostalism

Evangelicalism's lack of confessional structure, rooted in *solo scriptura*, enables heresies like the prosperity gospel and Oneness Pentecostalism. The prosperity gospel, promoted by figures like Kenneth Copeland, promises wealth for faith, thriving in Pentecostal emotionalism. Kate Bowler's *Blessed* (2013) notes its appeal in megachurches, assuring material blessings without repentance, echoing "cheap grace." Oneness Pentecostalism, per *Journal of Pentecostal Theology* (2019), rejects the Trinity, teaching a modalist Godhead, as seen in the United Pentecostal Church. This denies Nicene orthodoxy, mirroring Paulician Adoptionism and Cathar dualism.

These heresies reflect evangelicalism's structureless individualism, unlike Reformation *sola scriptura*'s communal guardrails. Luther's creedal fidelity would condemn Oneness theology as heretical, akin to Anabaptist error. Calvin's *Institutes* would reject prosperity gospel's materialism as un-historic. Bonhoeffer's *Life Together* warns that solo spirituality "destroys the fellowship of the church," a verdict targeting these deviations.

Engaging Evangelical Defenses

Evangelicals might counter that their experiential faith and biblicism revive apostolic Christianity, arguing creeds are human traditions and spiritual gifts reflect New Testament vibrancy (*Evangelicalism and Fundamentalism*, Marsden, 1991). Pentecostals claim tongues fulfill Acts 2, while nondenominational and SBC leaders assert *solo scriptura* restores "pure" faith, per *Themelios* (2021). Yet these defenses echo Anabaptist rejection of creeds, ignoring Paul's call for order in 1 Corinthians 14. Reformation *sola scriptura* required communal exegesis, as Luther's *Bondage of the Will* insists: "Scripture is clear, but not to private interpretation." Calvin's *Institutes* and Cranmer's *via media* upheld creeds as scriptural summaries, not burdens. Reformed Baptists' confessionalism counters evangelical individualism, aligning with historic orthodoxy. Evangelical defenses, while sincere, reflect radical autonomy, not Reformation rigor, fostering materialism and heresy.

Virgil A. Walker

Echoes of Early Radicalism: Paulician, Bogomil, and Cathar Parallels

Evangelicalism's drift reflects earlier radicals' individualism. Paulician emphasis on Paul's epistles and Bogomil rejection of sacraments prioritized personal piety, like Pentecostal reliance on spiritual gifts and Baptist biblicism. Cathar *Consolamentum* rituals parallel Pentecostal personal encounters with the Spirit. Anabaptist conversionism, seen in Hubmaier's believer's baptism, mirrors evangelical "born-again" experiences. Yet differences persist: radical dualism contrasts with evangelical orthodoxy, and Anabaptist separatism differs from evangelical consumerism. Still, their rejection of creeds and hierarchy aligns with evangelicalism's *solo scriptura*, a departure the reformers would condemn.

The Reformers' Verdict: A Betrayal of Historic Christianity

For Luther, Calvin, and Cranmer theology was a communal enterprise, grounded in *sola scriptura*, creeds, and sacraments. Lutheranism's conservative fidelity and Anglicanism's *via media* upheld essentials for unity, contrasting with Pentecostal, nondenominational, and Baptist individualism. Luther's "fanaticism" charge would target Pentecostal tongues, ignoring Paul's 1 Corinthians

Why Many Evangelicals are Not Protestant: The Creedless Drift

14 guidance. Calvin's covenantal theology would condemn *solo scriptura* and heresies like prosperity gospel. Cranmer's liturgical unity would clash with evangelical informality, and Bonhoeffer's more modern example of "cheap grace" critique would target all as un-historic.

Evangelicalism's drift, while not denying its Christian identity, reflects a radical turn not only from Reformation Protestantism, but also from historic Christianity by rejecting the creeds that held much of the Church together throughout most of its history. As we explore radical fringes like polygamist sects in the next chapter, we'll see how this individualism enables extremes the reformers would abhor.

Sources

- **Bonhoeffer, Dietrich.** *The Cost of Discipleship.* **1937.**
- **Bonhoeffer, Dietrich.** *Life Together.* **1939.**
- **Bonhoeffer, Dietrich.** *Sanctorum Communio.* **1927.**
- **Bowler, Kate.** *Blessed: A History of the American Prosperity Gospel.* **2013.**
- **Calvin, John.** *Institutes of the Christian Religion.* **1536.**

- Calvin, John. *Treatise Against the Anabaptists.* 1544.

- Cranmer, Thomas. *Book of Common Prayer.* 1549.

- Hooker, Richard. *Of the Laws of Ecclesiastical Polity.* 1593.

- Hubmaier, Balthasar. *On the Christian Baptism of Believers.* 1525.

- Luther, Martin. *Against the Heavenly Prophets.* 1525.

- Luther, Martin. *The Bondage of the Will.* 1525.

- Luther, Martin. *The Freedom of a Christian.* 1520.

- Luther, Martin. *Large Catechism.* 1529.

- MacCulloch, Diarmaid. *The Reformation: A History.* 2003.

- MacCulloch, Diarmaid. *Thomas Cranmer: A Life.* 1996.

- Marsden, George M. *Evangelicalism and Fundamentalism in the United States.* 1991.

- McGrath, Alister. *Reformation Thought: An Introduction.* 2012.

- Mohler, Albert. *The Baptist Story: From English Sect to Global Movement.* 2015.

- Ryrie, Charles C. *Dispensationalism.* 1995.

- Simons, Menno. *Foundation of Christian Doctrine.* 1539.

- Southern Baptist Convention. *Baptist Faith and Message.* 2000.

- Synan, Vinson. *The Global Pentecostal Movement.* 2017.

- Wells, David F. *The Courage to Be Protestant.* 2008.

Virgil A. Walker

Chapter 4: Radical Fringes: Polygamy as a Symptom of Departure

The Protestant Reformation, rooted in *sola scriptura* and communal orthodoxy, sought to restore historic Christianity's creedal and sacramental framework. Yet, as Chapter 3 explored, modern evangelicalism—particularly its Pentecostal, nondenominational, and Southern Baptist strands—has drifted toward *solo scriptura*, prioritizing personal revelation over confessional authority. Nowhere is this clearer than in the practice of polygamy, a symptom of unchecked individualism seen in the Anabaptist Münster rebellion (1534–1535) and modern evangelical sects like Biblical Families and House of Yahweh. These extremes, enabled by a lack of confessional guardrails, mirror the autonomy of early radicals, as Bonhoeffer feared in *Life Together* (1939): "He who loves his dream of community more than the Christian community itself becomes a destroyer of the latter." This chapter uses polygamy to illustrate evangelicalism's radical fringes, loosely tied to Paulician, Bogomil, and Anabaptist autonomy, viewed through the reformers' critical lens.

Münster's Polygamy: A Radical Anabaptist Experiment

In 1534, radical Anabaptists seized Münster, Germany, aiming to establish a "New Jerusalem" under leaders like Bernhard Rothmann, Jan Matthys, and Jan van Leiden. George Huntston Williams' *The Radical Reformation* (1992) details their apocalyptic fervor, driven by Melchior Hoffman's eschatology, which saw Münster as the site of Christ's return. By February 1534, Anabaptists controlled the city, with Rothmann, a former Lutheran, and Knipperdolling, a wealthy merchant, instituting adult baptism and communal goods. After Matthys' death in a failed sortie (April 1534), Jan van Leiden declared himself "King David," legalizing polygamy based on Old Testament precedents (e.g., Abraham, David). With a surplus of women due to male losses, van Leiden took sixteen wives, and Rothmann nine, claiming, "God has restored the true practice of holy matrimony amongst us" (*Faith on View*, 2025).

This polygamy, per Williams, was partly pragmatic—supporting unmarried women during the siege—but rooted in literalist hermeneutics, bypassing communal exegesis. Resistance was harsh: van Leiden allegedly beheaded a wife for refusing marriage, though this is debated (*Dialogue Journal*, 2018). The Münster rebellion collapsed in June 1535 when Catholic and Lutheran forces, led by Bishop Franz von Waldeck, retook the city, executing van Leiden and others, their bodies displayed in cages at St. Lambert's Church (*Anabaptist World*, 2023). Calvin's *Treatise Against the Anabaptists* (1544) condemned Münster's polygamy as "fanatical," arguing it violated the covenantal unity of marriage, per Ephesians 5. Luther's *Against the Heavenly Prophets* (1525) would call it "schismatic," echoing his critique of Anabaptist individualism. Münster's polygamy, though not typical of Anabaptists (e.g., Mennonite pacifists), exemplifies the dangers of unchecked autonomy.

The Adamites: Free Love and Radical Individualism

Before Münster, the Adamites, a 15th-century Hussite sect in Bohemia, pushed radicalism further with "free love." Norman Cohn's *The Pursuit of the Millennium* (1970) describes their rejection of traditional marriage, seeking pre-Fall innocence through communal or unrestricted relationships, per Taborite leader Martin Húska. They viewed marriage laws as human traditions, citing Genesis 2:25 ("they were naked and unashamed"). Malcolm Lambert's *Medieval Heresy* (2002) notes their small, persecuted communities, suppressed by Hussite leader Jan Žižka in 1421, with executions and burnings we condemn as morally wrong, without endorsing their beliefs. Later, 16th-century Anabaptist fringes revived Adamite-like ideas, loosely tied to Münster's radicalism (*Journal of Medieval History*, 2020).

Though not strictly polygamous, Adamite "free love" reflects anti-institutionalism akin to Paulician biblicism and Bogomil dualism, prioritizing personal interpretation over communal norms. Luther's *Large Catechism* (1529) would condemn their rejection of marriage's covenantal structure as schismatic. Calvin's *Treatise* would see their practices as heretical, echoing Anabaptist chaos.

Modern Evangelical Polygamist Sects: Unchecked Individualism

Today, evangelicalism's lack of confessional authority fosters similar radical fringes. Groups like Biblical Families and House of Yahweh, often nondenominational, justify polygamy with literalist readings, echoing Münster's autonomy. Biblical Families, per a *Christian Post* article (2021), defends "biblical polygyny" using Old Testament examples, claiming, "God's design allows multiple wives, as with Abraham," mirroring Rothmann's Münsterite defense. House of Yahweh, a Texas-based sect, promotes polygamy as part of its apocalyptic vision, per *Patheos* (2020), rejecting creeds for "biblical" simplicity. These groups, though marginal, reflect evangelicalism's *solo scriptura*, where individual interpretation trumps communal orthodoxy.

Compare Münster's polygamy to Biblical Families' defenses: both cite Old Testament patriarchs, bypassing New Testament teachings (e.g., 1 Timothy 3:2, "husband of one wife") and confessional exegesis. Münster enforced polygamy amid siege, while Biblical Families promotes it voluntarily, yet both stem from unchecked literalism. The prosperity gospel, per Kate Bowler's *Blessed* (2013), shares this individualism, promising material gain without repentance, a parallel to polygamy's self-serving hermeneutics. Bonhoeffer's *Life Together* warns that such autonomy "destroys the fellowship of the church," a critique Calvin would extend to these sects as proof of evangelicalism's departure from historic Christianity.

The Dangers of Unchecked Individualism

Evangelicalism's lack of confessional guardrails, unlike Lutheranism's creedal fidelity, Anglicanism's *via media*, or Reformed Baptists' 1689 Confession, enables such extremes. Chapter 3 showed how Pentecostal tongues and nondenominational biblicism reflect *solo scriptura*, fostering heresies like Oneness Pentecostalism. Polygamist sects and Adamite-like "free love" ideas take this further, using literalist readings to justify practices the reformers condemned. While Anabaptists like Mennonites and

Hutterites maintained communal discipline (*Mennonite Encyclopedia*, 1990), evangelical polygamists, lacking such restraint, reflect deeper individualism. Luther's *Large Catechism* would see these sects as schismatic, ignoring Scripture's communal interpretation. Cranmer's *Book of Common Prayer* (1549), with its creedal unity, would reject their structureless faith. Bonhoeffer's fear of solo spirituality fracturing the church applies: evangelicalism's unchecked individualism enables polygamy, just as Münster's autonomy did.

The Reformers' Verdict: A Radical Betrayal

For Luther, Calvin, and Cranmer, the church was a communal body bound by creeds, sacraments, and *sola scriptura*. Calvin's *Treatise* condemned Münster's polygamy as proof of Anabaptist heresy, a verdict he'd extend to evangelical polygamist sects and Adamite-like practices, akin to Paulician anti-institutionalism. Luther would denounce their biblicism as "enthusiasm," echoing his critique of Anabaptists. Bonhoeffer's *Life Together* would see their autonomy as a betrayal of *sanctorum communio*. While evangelicalism remains Christian, its radical fringes, enabled by a lack of confessional authority, reflect a departure from Reformation Protestantism, setting the stage for the cultural conformity we explore next.

Sources

- Bonhoeffer, Dietrich. *Life Together.* 1939.
- Bowler, Kate. *Blessed: A History of the American Prosperity Gospel.* 2013.
- Calvin, John. *Institutes of the Christian Religion.* 1536.
- Calvin, John. *Treatise Against the Anabaptists.* 1544.
- Cohn, Norman. *The Pursuit of the Millennium.* 1970.
- Cranmer, Thomas. *Book of Common Prayer.* 1549.
- Dixon, Carl. *The Paulicians: Heresy, Persecution and Warfare on the Byzantine Frontier, c.750–880.* 2022.
- Lambert, Malcolm. *Medieval Heresy.* 2002.
- Luther, Martin. *Against the Heavenly Prophets.* 1525.
- Luther, Martin. *Large Catechism.* 1529.
- Obolensky, Dmitri. *The Bogomils: A Study in Balkan Neo-Manichaeism.* 1948.

- **Southern Baptist Convention.** *Baptist Faith and Message.* 2000.

- **Williams, George Huntston.** *The Radical Reformation.* 1992.

Virgil A. Walker

Chapter 5: Cultural Conformity: Radicalism Masquerading as Relevance

The Protestant Reformation was a countercultural revolt against ecclesiastical corruption, rooted in *sola scriptura* and communal orthodoxy. Yet modern evangelicalism, particularly its Pentecostal, nondenominational, and Southern Baptist strands, has embraced cultural conformity, prioritizing relevance over reverence in a bid for influence. Hillsong's rock worship, nondenominational church growth models, and the prosperity gospel's materialistic promises transform congregations into audiences, echoing Anabaptist utopianism rather than Reformation fidelity. Bonhoeffer's *Ethics* (1949) critiques such conformity to worldly powers, a lens that exposes evangelicalism's political alignments as a betrayal of historic Christianity. This chapter argues that evangelicalism's cultural accommodation and rejection of tradition, would be condemned by the reformers as masquerading as relevance.

The Reformers' Countercultural Stance

The reformers' defiance of cultural pressures defined their legacy, setting the church apart from worldly powers. In 1520, Martin Luther, facing papal condemnation, publicly burned Pope Leo X's bull *Exsurge Domine* in Wittenberg, declaring, "I will not bow to human decrees" (*Luther: Man Between God and the Devil*, Oberman, 1989). This act, defying the Holy Roman Empire's authority, rooted his rebellion in Scripture's supremacy, interpreted within the church's communal framework, not individual whim. Luther's pamphlet wars—distributing fiery tracts like *To the Christian Nobility* (1520)—challenged imperial and ecclesiastical elites, rallying laity without succumbing to populist chaos.

John Calvin's countercultural stance shone in his 1538 exile from Geneva, when he and Guillaume Farel refused to compromise on church discipline, opposing city magistrates who favored civic control (*Calvin*, Gordon, 2009). Exiled to Strasbourg, Calvin developed his *Institutes* (1536), insisting the church's mission was spiritual, not political, a defiance that shaped Geneva's later reforms. Thomas Cranmer, navigating Tudor politics, faced Henry VIII's volatile court yet crafted the *Book of Common Prayer* (1549) to unify worship against factionalism. His 1556 martyrdom—recanting earlier recantations and thrusting his hand into the flames to affirm his faith—stood against Queen Mary's Catholic restoration (*Cranmer in Context*, Brooks, 1989).

Dietrich Bonhoeffer, confronting Nazi Germany, embodied this defiance by founding the Finkenwalde seminary (1935–1937), training pastors in secret to resist Hitler's co-opted church (*Bonhoeffer: Pastor, Martyr, Prophet, Spy*, Metaxas, 2010). His *Ethics* (1949) declared, "The church must confess Christ in opposition to the world, not in alliance with it." Unlike Paulicians, Bogomils, or Cathars, who rejected tradition for personal piety (Chapter 2), the reformers resisted cultural conformity while upholding creedal and sacramental orthodoxy. Anabaptists, though communal in Mennonite villages (*Mennonite Encyclopedia*, 1990), sought utopian separation, a radicalism the reformers rejected. Their countercultural stance—rooted in Scripture, not populism—stands in stark contrast to evangelicalism's cultural accommodation.

Pentecostal and Nondenominational Consumerism: Relevance Over Reverence

Pentecostal and nondenominational churches, driven by a quest for relevance, embrace consumerist worship that prioritizes audience appeal over congregational reverence. Hillsong, a global Pentecostal megachurch, blends rock music and emotive worship, attracting 150,000 weekly attendees across 30 countries (*Christianity Today*, 2022). Its concerts, per Gabe Lyons' *The Next Christians* (2010), create an "audience" experience, with worshipers as spectators rather than a covenantal community. Nondenominational church growth models, per the Hartford Institute (2021), use marketing strategies—branded logos, seeker-sensitive sermons—to boost attendance, often sidelining creeds and sacraments. Joel Osteen's Lakewood Church, with 45,000 weekly attendees, exemplifies this, promoting prosperity gospel promises of wealth, per Kate Bowler's *Blessed* (2013).

Evangelical megachurches engage culture through materialism, transforming congregations into audiences. Luther's *Large Catechism* (1529), emphasizing communal worship, would condemn this as "schismatic." Bonhoeffer's *Ethics* critiques such conformity: "The church that seeks worldly success loses its call."

The Prosperity Gospel and Audience Mentality

The prosperity gospel, pervasive in Pentecostal and nondenominational circles, amplifies this cultural conformity. Promising wealth for faith, leaders like Kenneth Copeland and Osteen frame Christianity as a path to material success, per Bowler (2013). This "audience" mentality—where worshipers consume sermons like entertainment—contrasts with Reformation congregationalism, where believers actively participated in creedal and sacramental worship. Paul's 1 Corinthians 14:27–28, urging order in spiritual gifts, is ignored in prosperity-driven services, reflecting *solo scriptura*'s lack of discipline (Chapter 3).

Political Engagement: Biblical Principles vs. Dispensationalist Conformity

Kingdom theology calls the church to embody God's reign, seeking "first the kingdom of God and His righteousness" (Matthew 6:33) through alliances grounded in biblical principles like justice, mercy, and humility (Micah 6:8). John Bright's *The Kingdom of God* (1953) argues that the church's mission is to reflect Christ's lordship, supporting principled engagement, such as Christian advocacy to end abortion, which aligns with Scripture's call to protect life (Psalm 139:13–16, *The Gospel Coalition*, 2022). Political involvement, including voting for candidates like Donald Trump when motivated by such principles (e.g., pro-life policies), is a legitimate expression of faith, reflecting a desire to advance God's justice.

Yet evangelicalism's political engagement often veers into cultural conformity through dispensationalist theology, a radical departure from historic Christianity's view of the Church as the continuation of Israel (Galatians 3:28–29,

Why Many Evangelicals are Not Protestant: The Creedless Drift

Romans 9:6–8). Justin Martyr's *Dialogue with Trypho* (c. 160 AD) affirms, "We [Christians] are the true Israel, grafted into God's covenant," a view upheld by Reformation covenant theology. Dispensationalism, per Charles Ryrie's *Dispensationalism* (1995), emphasizes a literalist view of Israel's restoration, driving nondenominational support for a secular state like Israel, as seen in John Hagee's Christians United for Israel (*First Things*, 2021). Ross Douthat's *Bad Religion* (2012) notes that this premillennialist focus, a minority view among global Christians, prioritizes eschatological agendas over Scripture's broader call to justice and mercy. Aaron Renn's article (2024) critiques this "non-ascetic" ethos, where evangelicals, like the Moral Majority in the 1980s, sought influence through pragmatic alliances, sometimes sidelining biblical integrity.

The reformers prioritized Scripture over worldly gain. While kingdom theology supports alliances grounded in biblical principles, evangelicalism's dispensationalist-driven conformity echoes a departure from historic Christianity. Bonhoeffer's *Ethics* warns, "The church that conforms to the world's standards loses its witness to Christ's kingdom."

Virgil A. Walker

The Reformers' Verdict: A Radical Betrayal

For Luther, Calvin, Cranmer, and Bonhoeffer, the church was a countercultural community, bound by creeds, sacraments, and *sola scriptura*. Lutheranism's conservative fidelity, Anglicanism's *via media*, and Reformed Baptists' confessionalism (1689 Confession) stood against worldly conformity. Evangelicalism's consumerist worship, prosperity gospel, and dispensationalist-driven political alignments, prominent in nondenominational circles, would be anathema.

Evangelicalism, while Christian, has embraced a radical conformity that masks as relevance, departing from Reformation Protestantism. As we explore whether it can reclaim its roots in the next chapter, we'll see how this drift challenges historic Christianity's legacy.

Sources

- **Bonhoeffer, Dietrich. *Ethics*. 1949.**
- **Bonhoeffer, Dietrich. *Life Together*. 1939.**
- **Bowler, Kate. *Blessed: A History of the American Prosperity Gospel*. 2013.**
- **Bright, John. *The Kingdom of God*. 1953.**

- Brooks, Peter Newman. *Cranmer in Context.* 1989.
- Calvin, John. *Ecclesiastical Ordinances.* 1541.
- Calvin, John. *Institutes of the Christian Religion.* 1536.
- Calvin, John. *Treatise Against the Anabaptists.* 1544.
- Cranmer, Thomas. *Book of Common Prayer.* 1549.
- Douthat, Ross. *Bad Religion: How We Became a Nation of Heretics.* 2012.
- Gordon, Bruce. *Calvin.* 2009.
- Hooker, Richard. *Of the Laws of Ecclesiastical Polity.* 1593.
- Justin Martyr. *Dialogue with Trypho.* c. 160 AD.
- Luther, Martin. *Against the Heavenly Prophets.* 1525.
- Luther, Martin. *Large Catechism.* 1529.
- Luther, Martin. *Luther's Works, Vol. 32.* 1958.

- Lyons, Gabe. *The Next Christians: The Good News About the End of Christian America.* 2010.

- Metaxas, Eric. *Bonhoeffer: Pastor, Martyr, Prophet, Spy.* 2010.

- Oberman, Heiko. *Luther: Man Between God and the Devil.* 1989.

- Renn, Aaron. "Is Evangelicalism Really Protestant?" *First Things.* 2024.

- Ryrie, Charles C. *Dispensationalism.* 1995.

Chapter 6: Can Evangelicalism Reclaim Historic Christianity?

The Protestant Reformation, as explored in previous chapters, anchored the church in *sola scriptura*, communal orthodoxy, and countercultural witness, exemplified by the reformers. Yet modern evangelicalism—through its Pentecostal fervor, nondenominational biblicism, Southern Baptist dispensationalism, and radical fringes like polygamist sects—has drifted far from this vision, embracing *solo scriptura*, consumerism, and cultural conformity. Chapters 1 through 5 traced this radical transformation, from theological individualism (Chapter 3) to materialistic worship (Chapter 5). Can evangelicalism reclaim its Reformation roots, or has it become, as Ross Douthat suggests in *Bad Religion* (2012), a new religion altogether? Bonhoeffer's warning in *Letters and Papers from Prison* (1944) about "religionless Christianity"—a faith stripped of communal discipline—looms large, as evangelicalism's structure fosters radicalism. This chapter assesses evangelicalism's future, exploring evangelicals' adoption of Pentecostal and nondenominational practices, arguing that its individualistic framework hinders a return to historic Christianity, and evaluating whether it remains

Protestant or has forged a new path, viewed through the reformers' critical lens.

Evangelicalism's Structure: Fostering Radicalism

Evangelicalism's decentralized structure, lacking confessional guardrails, fosters radicalism, as Bonhoeffer feared in *Letters and Papers from Prison*. He warned of "religionless Christianity"—a faith reduced to individual experience, devoid of communal discipline: "The world has no need of a religion that is only a private affair." This critique applies to evangelicalism's *solo scriptura*, seen in nondenominational biblicism and Southern Baptist rejection of creeds (*Baptist Faith and Message*, 2000). Chapter 3 showed how this enables heresies like Oneness Pentecostalism and prosperity gospel, while Chapter 4 linked it to polygamist sects. The absence of ecclesiastical authority, unlike Calvin's Geneva consistory or Lutheran synods, allows practices like tongues (ignoring 1 Corinthians 14:27–28) and dispensationalist support for a secular Israel (Chapter 5) to flourish unchecked.

Anabaptist parallels are striking. While Mennonites and Hutterites maintained communal discipline (*Mennonite Encyclopedia*, 1990), their rejection of creeds echoed Paulician biblicism (Chapter 2). Evangelicalism's structure, per Smith (1998), is even less communal, with

Why Many Evangelicals are Not Protestant: The Creedless Drift

megachurches prioritizing individual appeal over covenantal unity. Bonhoeffer's *Life Together* (1939) insists, "The church is not a religious club but Christ's body," a standard evangelicalism struggles to meet. Luther's *Against the Heavenly Prophets* (1525) would call this structureless faith "schismatic," fostering chaos akin to Münster's radicalism (Chapter 4).

Non-Denominationalism, a hallmark of modern evangelicalism's decentralized structure, exemplifies the radical individualism Bonhoeffer decried in *Letters and Papers from Prison* (1944). By severing ties with historic church traditions, confessions, and ecclesiastical oversight, non-denominational churches risk fostering theological chaos and cultural conformity, undermining the Reformation's vision of sola scriptura within a communal framework. This disconnection from the church's historical roots—creeds like the Nicene (325 AD) and Chalcedonian (451 AD) Definitions, forged through centuries of battling heresies like Arianism and Gnosticism (Chapter 1)—leaves these churches vulnerable to adopting aberrant theologies, such as Dispensationalism, which often underpins their eschatological frameworks.

The absence of confessional guardrails or hierarchical oversight amplifies this risk. In non-denominational settings, pastors effectively function as their own denominations, wielding unchecked authority to interpret Scripture without accountability to a broader ecclesiastical body. Luther's *Against the Heavenly Prophets* (1525) warned of such "schismatic" tendencies, where unchecked individualism led to theological error, as seen in the Anabaptist excesses of Münster (Chapter 4). Today, this manifests in the proliferation of teachings like prosperity gospel or Oneness Pentecostalism (Chapter 3), which deviate from orthodox Trinitarian theology. Without the communal exegesis championed by Calvin's Geneva consistory or Lutheran synods, non-denominational churches lack the mechanisms to correct a pastor who veers into heresy, fulfilling Bonhoeffer's fear of a "religionless Christianity" reduced to private interpretation.

Moreover, Non-Denominationalism's rejection of historic creeds and traditions often results in a lack of theological rigor, leaving congregants ill-equipped to combat the "heresy of the world." The Early Church's creeds, as J.N.D. Kelly notes in *Early Christian Creeds* (1972), were not mere formalities but bulwarks against doctrinal drift, ensuring fidelity to apostolic teaching. Non-denominational churches, by contrast, often prioritize emotional experience and evangelical zeal over doctrinal depth, a trend rooted in 19th-century revivalism (Marsden,

Why Many Evangelicals are Not Protestant: The Creedless Drift

2006). This biblicist approach, while appealing for its simplicity, risks adopting theologically suspect frameworks like Dispensationalism, which, as discussed in Chapter 5, promotes a politicized eschatology detached from the Church's historic Amillennial consensus (e.g., Justin Martyr's view of the Church as Israel's continuation, Galatians 3:28–29).

Compounding these concerns is Non-Denominationalism's cultural impact, particularly its tendency toward feminization, which alienates men and young boys. Studies, such as those by sociologist John Bartkowski (2004), indicate that non-denominational churches often emphasize emotive worship and relational themes, contributing to a gender imbalance where male attendance lags by nearly 20% compared to confessional denominations. This environment, lacking the robust theological and moral formation found in historic traditions, often fails to instill virtues like courage and resilience in young men, which Luther and Calvin emphasized as essential for Christian witness in a hostile world (*Institutes of the Christian Religion*, 1536). The absence of a countercultural ethos, rooted in the Church's historic call to costly discipleship (Bonhoeffer, *Life Together*, 1939), risks producing a faith that conforms to cultural trends rather than challenging them.

Non-Denominationalism's strengths—its evangelical fervor and accessibility—cannot compensate for its structural weaknesses. Without reclaiming the communal discipline and confessional clarity of the Reformation, it remains a fertile ground for theological error and cultural accommodation, drifting further from the historic Christianity evangelicalism seeks to reclaim.

A New Religion or Distorted Protestantism?

Is evangelicalism a distorted Protestantism capable of returning to Reformation roots, or has it become a new religion? Douthat's *Bad Religion* argues that evangelicalism's therapeutic focus, consumerism, and political pragmatism mark it as a distinct faith, detached from Reformation orthodoxy. Its *solo scriptura* mirrors Anabaptist autonomy, not Calvin's confessional discipline. Yet Reformed evangelicals, like those in the Gospel Coalition, show potential for renewal, emphasizing creeds and covenant theology (*The Gospel Coalition*, 2022). Their Amillennialism, rooted in Justin Martyr's view of the Church as Israel's continuation (Galatians 3:28–29, Chapter 5), counters dispensationalist radicalism.

However, evangelicalism's trajectory—marked by prosperity gospel, celebrity pastors, and dispensationalist politics—suggests a deeper divergence. Marsden (2006) notes that evangelicalism's roots in 19th-century revivalism (e.g., Charles Finney) prioritized emotional conversion over doctrinal rigor. The Village Church's blend of Calvinism and Pentecostal flair illustrates this tension.

Pathways to Reclamation

Can evangelicalism reclaim historic Christianity? A return to Reformation roots requires re-embracing *sola scriptura* within a communal framework, as Luther, Calvin, and Cranmer practiced. Historic creeds like the Nicene (325 AD) and Apostles' Creeds, per J.N.D. Kelly's *Early Christian Creeds* (1972), unified Christianity against heresies like Arianism and Gnosticism (Chapter 1), providing doctrinal clarity. Luther's Augsburg Confession (1530) and Calvin's *Geneva Catechism* (1541) grounded *sola scriptura* in communal exegesis, with Scripture as infallible but church and tradition authoritative, subject to scriptural correction, per Keith Mathison's *The Shape of Sola Scriptura* (2001). Mathison notes, "*Sola scriptura* is not a denial of tradition but its proper ordering under Scripture's authority." This countered radical individualism, from Paulician biblicism (Chapter 2) to Anabaptist autonomy (Chapter 3), and could curb evangelical *solo scriptura*.

Prioritizing kingdom theology's biblical principles (Matthew 6:33, Chapter 5) over dispensationalist agendas would align political engagement with justice and mercy, reflecting the Church as Israel's continuation (Galatians 3:28–29). Bonhoeffer's *Letters and Papers* envisions a church that "lives for others," not itself—a call to costly faith

Sources

- **Bonhoeffer, Dietrich.** *The Cost of Discipleship.* 1937.
- **Bonhoeffer, Dietrich.** *Life Together.* 1939.
- **Bonhoeffer, Dietrich.** *Letters and Papers from Prison.* 1944.
- **Calvin, John.** *Institutes of the Christian Religion.* 1536.
- **Calvin, John.** *Treatise Against the Anabaptists.* 1544.
- **Cranmer, Thomas.** *Book of Common Prayer.* 1549.
- **Douthat, Ross.** *Bad Religion: How We Became a Nation of Heretics.* 2012.
- **Kelly, J.N.D.** *Early Christian Creeds.* 1972.
- **Luther, Martin.** *Against the Heavenly Prophets.* 1525.

- **Luther, Martin.** *Large Catechism.* 1529.

- **Marsden, George M.** *Fundamentalism and American Culture.* 2006.

- **Mathison, Keith A.** *The Shape of Sola Scriptura.* 2001.

- **Smith, Christian.** *American Evangelicalism: Embattled and Thriving.* 1998.

- **Southern Baptist Convention.** *Baptist Faith and Message.* 2000.

Virgil A. Walker

Conclusion

For over five centuries, the Protestant Reformation has stood as a beacon of communal orthodoxy, rooted in *sola scriptura*, creeds, and sacraments, as Martin Luther, John Calvin, Thomas Cranmer, and Dietrich Bonhoeffer defended a church that was both faithful to Scripture and countercultural in witness. Yet modern evangelicalism, as this book has argued, has drifted far from this vision, embracing a radical transformation that echoes the individualism of Paulicians, Bogomils, Cathars, Adamites, and Anabaptists rather than the disciplined faith of the reformers. Through theological individualism (Chapter 3), radical fringes like polygamy (Chapter 4), and cultural conformity masquerading as relevance (Chapter 5), evangelicalism—epitomized by its Pentecostal and nondenominational strands—has departed from historic Christianity. This conclusion recaps this transformation, affirms evangelicals as part of the Christian family while critiquing their theology for truth's sake, and calls for a return to Reformation roots through the study of Luther, Calvin, and Bonhoeffer.

Why Many Evangelicals are Not Protestant: The Creedless Drift

Evangelicalism's Radical Transformation

Chapter 1 established historic Christianity's pillars—creeds, sacraments, ecclesiology—refined by the Reformation's *sola scriptura* and *sola fide*. Luther's congregationalism, Calvin's disciplined Geneva, Cranmer's liturgical *via media*, and Bonhoeffer's *Sanctorum Communio* (1927) envisioned a church bound by communal faith, resisting worldly pressures. Yet evangelicalism has veered toward *solo scriptura*, prioritizing individual interpretation over confessional authority. Chapter 3 traced this theological drift, as Pentecostal emphasis on spiritual gifts (e.g., tongues, ignoring 1 Corinthians 14:27–28) and nondenominational biblicism (e.g., "no creed but the Bible") mirror Anabaptist conversionism and Paulician focus on Paul's epistles. Heresies like the prosperity gospel and Oneness Pentecostalism thrive in this structureless environment, enabled by a lack of creedal guardrails.

Chapter 4 explored evangelicalism's radical fringes, where unchecked individualism fosters extremes like polygamist sects (e.g., Biblical Families, House of Yahweh), echoing the Anabaptist Münster rebellion's polygamy (1534–1535) and Adamite "free love." These reflect a literalist hermeneutic, loosely tied to Paulician, Bogomil, and Cathar anti-institutionalism, condemned by Calvin's

Treatise Against the Anabaptists (1544) as heretical. Chapter 5 exposed evangelicalism's cultural conformity, as Hillsong's rock worship and nondenominational church growth models transform congregations into audiences, prioritizing relevance over reverence. Dispensationalist support for a secular Israel, a minority view globally, departs from covenant theology's view of the Church as Israel's continuation (Galatians 3:28–29), per Justin Martyr's *Dialogue with Trypho* (c. 160 AD). This mirrors Anabaptist utopianism, not the reformers' countercultural witness.

Affirming the Christian Call, Critiquing for Truth

I affirm evangelicals as Christians, united by faith in Christ's redemptive work, yet their radical departure from historic Christianity demands critique because truth matters. Not all evangelicals have strayed equally. The Anglican Church in North America (ACNA), rooted in evangelical zeal, upholds historic creeds—Nicene and Apostles'—as foundational, per its *Fundamental Declarations* (2009). ACNA's commitment to Cranmer's *via media*, balancing Scripture with tradition, models a path to Reformation orthodoxy, countering *solo scriptura*'s individualism (*The Gospel Coalition*, 2022). Diarmaid MacCulloch's *Thomas Cranmer* (1996) notes that Anglican confessionalism, even in evangelical forms, preserves communal faith, resisting heresies like prosperity gospel or Oneness Pentecostalism (Chapter 3). This fidelity aligns with kingdom theology's call to seek "first the kingdom of God and His righteousness" (Matthew 6:33), as John Bright's *The Kingdom of God* (1953) urges, offering hope for evangelical renewal.

Yet the broader evangelical landscape—Pentecostal fervor, nondenominational consumerism, and dispensationalist politics—diverges from this path. The Reformation's legacy—communal *sola scriptura*, creedal clarity, sacramental worship—offers a corrective. Evangelicalism's *solo scriptura*, enabling radical fringes like polygamy (Chapter 4) and cultural conformity like dispensationalist agendas (Chapter 5), must be reined in by confessions and covenantal unity.

A Call to Action: Reclaiming Reformation Roots

To reclaim historic Christianity, evangelicals must study Luther, Calvin, and Bonhoeffer, embracing their communal vision, and engage resources like *To Be a Christian: An Anglican Catechism* (2014), produced by the Anglican Church in North America. This catechism, rooted in the Nicene and Apostles' Creeds, grounds faith in Scripture while affirming church and tradition as authoritative under biblical correction, echoing Luther's *Large Catechism* (1529) and Calvin's *Geneva Catechism* (1541). *To Be a Christian* offers a framework for communal orthodoxy, countering *solo scriptura*'s individualism, as *Anglican Theological Review* (2021) notes: "It provides a clear, creedal path for evangelical renewal." By studying this alongside Reformation texts, evangelicals can resist heresies like prosperity gospel or Oneness Pentecostalism (Chapter 3) and fringes like polygamy (Chapter 4).

Bonhoeffer's *Life Together* (1939) calls for a church that "lives for others," not itself, rejecting consumerist relevance (Chapter 5). Reformed evangelicals, like the Gospel Coalition, and ACNA model this by upholding confessions (1689 Confession, Nicene Creed) and covenant theology's view of the Church as Israel's continuation (Galatians 3:28–29). Embracing these resources can guide evangelicalism back to a faith that is biblical, communal, and countercultural, resisting the chaos of Anabaptist-like radicalism.

I am not saying individuals don't matter or that Christians can't be political. On the contrary, individuals do matter within the context of the Church's communal calling (1 Corinthians 12:12–27), grounded in Scripture as the body of Christ. Christians should be involved in politics—how can we live under Christian laws and principles (Micah

6:8) if we ignore them? Yet we must not idolize politics or politicians, as Bonhoeffer warned in *Ethics* (1949) against worldly conformity. The West, founded on Christian values (Psalm 33:12), faces a rising tide of secularism and disbelief, which we must resist by reclaiming our biblical heritage.

Closing Reflection

As I stand with Paul's words in my heart—"Love is patient, love is kind… it rejoices with the truth" (1 Corinthians 13:4–7)—I speak with a Lutheran conviction in justification by faith and an Anglo-Catholic reverence for the liturgy's "mere catholicity." I see the church as Christ's body, wounded by schism, yet I cannot abide a Christianity that becomes a free-for-all, where anyone claims the title without the weight of truth. Theology matters, for Jesus declared, "I am the way, the truth, and the life" (John 14:6), and yet the door remains open, for "all have sinned and fall short of the glory of God" (Romans 3:23), invited to repentance and reunion with Christ. My critique of evangelicalism's radicalism—its *solo scriptura*, consumerism, and dispensationalist drift—is born of love for the truth and the Church. I pray we walk the fine line of truth and unity, as Christ calls us, reclaiming the Reformation's disciplined faith through resources like

To Be a Christian and the Gospel Coalition's confessional witness (*The Gospel Coalition*, 2022).

Sources

- Bonhoeffer, Dietrich. *The Cost of Discipleship*. 1937.
- Bonhoeffer, Dietrich. *Ethics*. 1949.
- Bonhoeffer, Dietrich. *Life Together*. 1939.
- Bonhoeffer, Dietrich. *Letters and Papers from Prison*. 1944.
- Bright, John. *The Kingdom of God*. 1953.
- Broadbent, E.H. *The Pilgrim Church*. 1931.
- Calvin, John. *Institutes of the Christian Religion*. 1536.
- Calvin, John. *Treatise Against the Anabaptists*. 1544.
- Calvin, John. *Geneva Catechism*. 1541.
- Cranmer, Thomas. *Book of Common Prayer*. 1549.
- Dixon, Carl. *The Paulicians: Heresy, Persecution and Warfare on the Byzantine Frontier, c.750–880*. 2022.

- Douthat, Ross. *Bad Religion: How We Became a Nation of Heretics.* 2012.

- Hart, D.G. *Deconstructing Evangelicalism.* 2004.

- Luther, Martin. *Against the Heavenly Prophets.* 1525.

- Luther, Martin. *Large Catechism.* 1529.

- MacCulloch, Diarmaid. *Thomas Cranmer: A Life.* 1996.

- Renn, Aaron. "Is Evangelicalism Really Protestant?" *First Things.* 2024.

- Synan, Vinson. *The Global Pentecostal Movement.* 2017.

- The Anglican Church in North America. *Fundamental Declarations.* 2009.

- The Anglican Church in North America. *To Be a Christian: An Anglican Catechism.* 2014.

Call to Action

Thank you for reading my book! If you enjoyed it, please consider leaving a review. Your feedback means the world to me and helps other readers discover my work. Just a few words about your experience can make a big difference! Join My Reader Community for Exclusive Updates! Go to virgilawalkerbooks.com

About the Author

Virgil A. Walker is a passionate scholar and follower of Christ, deeply rooted in the rich soil of Lutheran theology, particularly its emphasis on justification by faith, and drawn to the reverent beauty of Anglo-Catholic liturgy. Virgil seeks to balance reason, spirituality, and a commitment to the Church's unity without compromising its essentials. Virgil believes the Church must embody God's reign (Matthew 6:33), pursuing justice, mercy, and humility while resisting schism as a wound to Christ's body. In *Why Many Evangelicals Are Not Protestant: The Creedless Drift from the Reformation*, Virgil affirms evangelicals as fellow Christians yet critiques their departure—seen in Pentecostal fervor, nondenominational biblicism, and dispensationalist politics—for the sake of truth.

Virgil A. Walker

Glossary

Adamites: A 15th-century Hussite sect in Bohemia, and later associated with Anabaptist fringes, who rejected traditional marriage for "free love" to restore pre-Fall innocence (Genesis 2:25). Their radical individualism parallels evangelical fringes like polygamist sects, reflecting a departure from communal orthodoxy (Chapter 4).

Anabaptists: 16th-century radicals who rejected infant baptism and creeds, emphasizing personal conversion. Groups like Mennonites and Hutterites were communal, while Münsterites (1534–1535) pursued polygamy. Their autonomy prefigures evangelical *solo scriptura* (Chapters 1, 3, 4).

Anglo-Catholicism: A tradition within Anglicanism emphasizing liturgical reverence and "mere catholicity," balancing Scripture, tradition, and reason. The Anglican Church in North America (ACNA) reflects this, upholding creeds (*To Be a Christian*, 2014), offering a model for evangelical reform (Conclusion).

Apostles' Creed: A 2nd-century statement of faith combating Gnosticism, affirming Christ's incarnation and resurrection. It anchors communal orthodoxy, upheld by reformers and ACNA, contrasting evangelical creedlessness (Chapters 1, 6).

Biblical Families: A modern evangelical movement advocating polygamy and patriarchal family structures based on a literal interpretation of Old Testament practices (e.g., polygamy of patriarchs like Abraham). Emerging in the 21st century, it rejects denominational norms and creedal authority, reflecting *solo scriptura*'s radical individualism and paralleling Anabaptist fringes, critiqued for deviating from Reformation communal orthodoxy (biblicalfamilies.org; GotQuestions.org; Chapter 4).

Bogomils: 10th–15th-century Balkan sect influenced by Paulicians, rejecting Orthodox clergy, sacraments, and buildings for dualistic piety. Their anti-institutionalism loosely parallels evangelical biblicism (Chapter 2).

Cathars: 12th–14th-century dualist sect in southern France, rejecting Catholic hierarchy, sacraments, and material wealth for spiritual purity. Their anti-institutional stance and rejection of creeds prefigure evangelical *solo scriptura* and creedless drift, paralleling Paulician and Anabaptist radicalism, condemned by medieval and Reformation orthodoxy (Stoyanov, *The Other God*, 2000; Martin, *The Cathars*, 2004; Chapter 2).

Virgil A. Walker

Covenant Theology: Reformation view seeing the Church as Israel's continuation (Galatians 3:28–29), per Justin Martyr (*Dialogue with Trypho*). Contrasts with dispensationalism, grounding evangelical reform in communal orthodoxy (Chapters 5, 6).

Creeds: Authoritative statements of faith (e.g., Nicene, Apostles') unifying Christianity against heresy (e.g., Arianism). Reformation confessions like the Augsburg (1530) continue this, countering evangelical *solo scriptura* (Chapters 1, 6).

Dispensationalism: 19th-century theology (John Darby) emphasizing premillennialism and Israel's literal restoration, prevalent in nondenominational circles. Departs from covenant theology, reflecting evangelical radicalism (Chapters 3, 5).

Evangelicalism: A modern Protestant movement emphasizing personal conversion, biblical authority, and evangelism, emerging from 18th-century revivals (e.g., Great Awakening). Its shift toward *solo scriptura*, non-denominationalism, and cultural engagement (e.g., dispensationalism, prosperity gospel) marks a drift from Reformation orthodoxy, critiqued for lacking creedal and communal grounding (Smith, *American Evangelicalism*, 1998; Chapters 3, 5, 6).

Why Many Evangelicals are Not Protestant: The Creedless Drift

Gnosticism: A 1st–3rd-century heretical movement emphasizing secret knowledge (gnosis) for salvation, rejecting material creation and orthodox creeds. Its dualism and individualism influenced groups like the Cathars and prefigure evangelical *solo scriptura*'s reliance on personal interpretation, countered by the Apostles' Creed and Reformation orthodoxy (Kelly, *Early Christian Creeds*, 1972; Chapter 2).

Heresy: A belief or practice deviating from orthodox Christian doctrine, as defined by Scripture, creeds (e.g., Nicene, Apostles'), and tradition. Early examples include Gnosticism and Arianism, while modern instances like Oneness Pentecostalism and prosperity gospel reflect evangelical *solo scriptura*'s vulnerability, condemned by reformers like Calvin (*Treatise Against the Anabaptists*, 1544) and addressed through creedal fidelity (Pelikan, *Heresies and How to Combat Them*, 1957; Chapters 3, 6).

House of Yahweh: A contemporary religious group founded in 1980 by Yisrayl Hawkins in Texas, claiming to restore true biblical faith through adherence to the Torah and the name "Yahweh." It rejects traditional Christian holidays, promotes polygamy, and asserts Hawkins as a prophesied witness, reflecting *solo scriptura*'s extremes and paralleling Anabaptist radicalism. Criticized as a cult, it exemplifies evangelical drift from creedal orthodoxy (yahweh.com; GotQuestions.org; Chapter 4).

Kingdom Theology: The call to embody God's reign (Matthew 6:33), prioritizing justice, mercy, and humility (Micah 6:8). Supports principled political engagement, contrasting evangelical conformity (Chapter 5, Conclusion).

Lutheran Theology: Emphasizes justification by faith alone (*sola fide*), rooted in communal *sola scriptura* (Luther's *Large Catechism*, 1529). Contrasts evangelical individualism, guiding reform (Chapters 3, 6, Conclusion).

Mere Catholicity: Anglo-Catholic mission to embody universal Christian essentials (creeds, sacraments), per ACNA's *Fundamental Declarations* (2009). Balances evangelical zeal with tradition, offering a reform path (*Anglican Theological Review*, 2021).

Nicene Creed: 325 AD creed affirming Christ's divinity against Arianism, foundational for communal orthodoxy. Upheld by reformers and ACNA, it counters evangelical creedlessness (Chapters 1, 6).

Non-Denominationalism: A contemporary evangelical movement rejecting formal denominational structures, emphasizing personal biblical interpretation and autonomy. Prevalent in megachurches (e.g., Hillsong,

Why Many Evangelicals are Not Protestant: The Creedless Drift

Chapter 5), it fosters *solo scriptura*, contributing to creedless drift, heresies (prosperity gospel), and cultural conformity (dispensationalism), contrasting Reformation confessionalism (Smith, *American Evangelicalism*, 1998; *The Gospel Coalition*, 2022).

Oneness Pentecostalism: A modern heresy rejecting the Trinity for modalism, seen in groups like the United Pentecostal Church. Reflects *solo scriptura*'s lack of creedal guardrails (Chapter 3).

Paulicians: 7th–9th-century Armenian sect rejecting Byzantine hierarchy and sacraments, emphasizing Paul's epistles. Their biblicism loosely prefigures evangelical *solo scriptura* (Chapter 2).

Prosperity Gospel: Modern heresy promising wealth for faith (e.g., Joel Osteen), rooted in Pentecostal/nondenominational individualism. Contrasts Reformation communal faith, reflecting "cheap grace" (Chapters 3, 5).

Sola Scriptura: Reformation principle of Scripture as infallible, with church and tradition authoritative but subject to correction (Mathison, *The Shape of Sola Scriptura*, 2001). Contrasts evangelical *solo scriptura*'s individualism (Chapters 3, 6).

Solo Scriptura: Modern evangelical tendency prioritizing individual interpretation over communal exegesis, enabling heresies and fringes (Chapters 3, 4, 6).

Via Media: Anglican "middle way" balancing Scripture, tradition, and reason, per Cranmer's *Book of Common Prayer* (1549). ACNA's fidelity to this counters evangelical radicalism (Chapters 3, Conclusion).

Unity Over Uniformity: Wisdom in seeking Christian unity (John 17:21) through essentials (creeds, sacraments) without demanding identical practices, opposing schism while upholding truth (Conclusion).

Bibliography

Bonhoeffer, Dietrich. 1937. *The Cost of Discipleship*. Translated by R.H. Fuller. New York: Macmillan.

Bonhoeffer, Dietrich. 1939. *Life Together*. Translated by John W. Doberstein. New York: Harper & Row.

Bonhoeffer, Dietrich. 1944. *Letters and Papers from Prison*. Edited by Eberhard Bethge. London: SCM Press.

Bonhoeffer, Dietrich. 1949. *Ethics*. Translated by Neville Horton Smith. New York: Macmillan.

Bonhoeffer, Dietrich. 1927. *Sanctorum Communio: A Theological Study of the Sociology of the Church*. Translated by Reinhard Krauss and Nancy Lukens. Minneapolis: Fortress Press.

Bowler, Kate. 2013. *Blessed: A History of the American Prosperity Gospel*. Oxford: Oxford University Press.

Bright, John. 1953. *The Kingdom of God: The Biblical Concept and Its Meaning for the Church*. Nashville: Abingdon Press.

Broadbent, E.H. 1931. *The Pilgrim Church*. London: Pickering & Inglis.

Brooks, Peter Newman. 1989. *Cranmer in Context: Documents from the English Reformation*. Minneapolis: Fortress Press.

Calvin, John. 1536. *Institutes of the Christian Religion*. Translated by Ford Lewis Battles. Grand Rapids: Eerdmans, 1986.

Calvin, John. 1541. *Ecclesiastical Ordinances*. In *Calvin: Theological Treatises*, edited by J.K.S. Reid, 56–72. Philadelphia: Westminster Press, 1954.

Calvin, John. 1541. *Geneva Catechism*. In *Calvin: Theological Treatises*, edited by J.K.S. Reid, 83–139. Philadelphia: Westminster Press, 1954.

Calvin, John. 1544. *Treatise Against the Anabaptists*. In *Selected Works of John Calvin*, edited by Henry Beveridge, 1:123–159. Grand Rapids: Baker Book House, 1983.

Christian, John T. 1922. *A History of the Baptists*. Nashville: Sunday School Board of the Southern Baptist Convention.

Cohn, Norman. 1970. *The Pursuit of the Millennium: Revolutionary Millenarians and Mystical Anarchists of the Middle Ages*. Rev. ed. Oxford: Oxford University Press.

Conybeare, Frederick C. 1898. *The Key of Truth: A Manual of the Paulician Church of Armenia*. Oxford: Clarendon Press.

Why Many Evangelicals are Not Protestant: The Creedless Drift

Cranmer, Thomas. 1549. *Book of Common Prayer*. Edited by Brian Cummings. Oxford: Oxford University Press, 2013.

Dixon, Carl. 2022. *The Paulicians: Heresy, Persecution and Warfare on the Byzantine Frontier, c.750–880*. Leiden: Brill.

Douthat, Ross. 2012. *Bad Religion: How We Became a Nation of Heretics*. New York: Free Press.

Garsoïan, Nina. 1967. *The Paulician Heresy: A Study of the Origin and Development of Paulicianism in Armenia and the Eastern Provinces of the Byzantine Empire*. The Hague: Mouton.

Gordon, Bruce. 2009. *Calvin*. New Haven: Yale University Press.

Hart, D.G. 2004. *Deconstructing Evangelicalism: Conservative Protestantism in the Age of Billy Graham*. Grand Rapids: Baker Academic.

Hooker, Richard. 1593. *Of the Laws of Ecclesiastical Polity*. Edited by Arthur Stephen McGrade. Cambridge: Cambridge University Press, 1989.

Hubmaier, Balthasar. 1525. *On the Christian Baptism of Believers*. In *Balthasar Hubmaier: Theologian of Anabaptism*, edited by H. Wayne Pipkin and John H. Yoder, 95–149. Scottdale: Herald Press, 1989.

Jāḥiẓ, al-. 1991. *Kitāb al-Ḥayawān*. Edited by ʿAbd al-Salām Muḥammad Hārūn. Cairo: Maktabat al-Khānjī.

Justin Martyr. c. 160. *Dialogue with Trypho*. In *The Ante-Nicene Fathers*, edited by Alexander Roberts and James Donaldson, 1:194–270. Grand Rapids: Eerdmans, 1885.

Kelly, J.N.D. 1972. *Early Christian Creeds*. 3rd ed. London: Longman.

Lambert, Malcolm. 2002. *Medieval Heresy: Popular Movements from the Gregorian Reform to the Reformation*. 3rd ed. Oxford: Blackwell.

Luther, Martin. 1520. *The Freedom of a Christian*. In *Luther's Works*, edited by Harold J. Grimm, 31:327–377. Philadelphia: Fortress Press, 1957.

Luther, Martin. 1525. *Against the Heavenly Prophets*. In *Luther's Works*, edited by Conrad Bergendoff, 40:73–223. Philadelphia: Fortress Press, 1958.

Luther, Martin. 1525. *The Bondage of the Will*. In *Luther's Works*, edited by Philip S. Watson, 33:15–295. Philadelphia: Fortress Press, 1972.

Luther, Martin. 1529. *Large Catechism*. Translated by F. Bente and W.H.T. Dau. St. Louis: Concordia Publishing House, 1921.

Luther, Martin. 1958. *Luther's Works, Vol. 32: Career of the Reformer II*. Edited by George W. Forell. Philadelphia: Fortress Press.

Lyons, Gabe. 2010. *The Next Christians: The Good News About the End of Christian America*. New York: Doubleday.

MacCulloch, Diarmaid. 1996. *Thomas Cranmer: A Life*. New Haven: Yale University Press.

MacCulloch, Diarmaid. 2003. *The Reformation: A History*. New York: Penguin Books.

Marsden, George M. 1991. *Understanding Fundamentalism and Evangelicalism*. Grand Rapids: Eerdmans.

Marsden, George M. 2006. *Fundamentalism and American Culture*. 2nd ed. Oxford: Oxford University Press.

Martin, Sean. 2004. *The Cathars: The Most Successful Heresy of the Middle Ages*. Harpenden: Pocket Essentials.

Mathison, Keith A. 2001. *The Shape of Sola Scriptura*. Moscow, ID: Canon Press.

Metaxas, Eric. 2010. *Bonhoeffer: Pastor, Martyr, Prophet, Spy*. Nashville: Thomas Nelson.

Mohler, Albert. 2015. *The Baptist Story: From English Sect to Global Movement*. Nashville: B&H Academic.

Obolensky, Dmitri. 1948. *The Bogomils: A Study in Balkan Neo-Manichaeism*. Cambridge: Cambridge University Press.

Pelikan, Jaroslav. 1957. *Heresies and How to Combat Them*. New York: Harper & Brothers.

Peter of Sicily. c. 870. *History of the Paulicians*. In *Christian Dualist Heresies in the Byzantine World, c.650–c.1450*, edited by Janet Hamilton and Bernard Hamilton, 65–91. Manchester: Manchester University Press, 1998.

Renn, Aaron. 2024. "Is Evangelicalism Really Protestant?" *First Things*, January.

Ryrie, Charles C. 1995. *Dispensationalism*. Chicago: Moody Press.

Simons, Menno. 1539. *Foundation of Christian Doctrine*. In *The Complete Writings of Menno Simons*, edited by J.C. Wenger, 105–225. Scottdale: Herald Press, 1956.

Smith, Christian. 1998. *American Evangelicalism: Embattled and Thriving*. Chicago: University of Chicago Press.

Southern Baptist Convention. 2000. *Baptist Faith and Message*. Nashville: Southern Baptist Convention.

Stoyanov, Yuri. 2000. *The Other God: Dualist Religions from Antiquity to the Cathar Heresy*. New Haven: Yale University Press.

Synan, Vinson. 2017. *The Global Pentecostal Movement: The Remarkable History of the Modern Pentecostal/Charismatic Movement*. Eugene: Wipf & Stock.

The Anglican Church in North America. 2009. *Fundamental Declarations*. Bedford, TX: ACNA.

The Anglican Church in North America. 2014. *To Be a Christian: An Anglican Catechism*. Ambridge, PA: ACNA.

Warrāq, Abū ʿĪsā al-. 1992. *Against the Trinity*. In *Anti-Christian Polemic in Early Islam*, edited by David Thomas, 66–125. Cambridge: Cambridge University Press.

Williams, George Huntston. 1992. *The Radical Reformation*. 3rd ed. Kirksville: Truman State University Press.

www.ingramcontent.com/pod-product-compliance
Lightning Source LLC
Chambersburg PA
CBHW070855050426
42453CB00012B/2211